90 YEARS AND STILL GOING STRONG

Linda Hudson Hoagland

PublishAmerica
Baltimore

First printing

PublishAmerica has allowed this work to remain exactly as the author intended, verbatim, without editorial input.

Photo used in cover art provided by Miranda Prather.

Softcover 9781462610822
PUBLISHED BY PUBLISHAMERICA, LLLP
www.publishamerica.com
Baltimore

Printed in the United States of America

PART I

CHAPTER 1

THE YEARS BEFORE STANLEY

"Why can't I go to school?" I pleaded with my father.

"School is evil. They fill your mind with bad things," he answered angrily to the same question I am sure my brothers and sisters had asked after the middle daughter was born. None of us were permitted to go to school. We weren't permitted to learn to read or write.

I was the tenth child of thirteen children born to Daniel Graham Holcomb who was an extremely religious fanatic. He would do anything possible for his neighbors to get praise that he was a good man, yet at home he was a tyrant, an extremely cruel person, showing no love whatsoever.

We were not permitted to go to church because we were told that churches only taught evil and that the churches were evil and the preachers were evil.

The religion that he belonged to didn't have a name; it was just a group of people that met. I guess you might call it a cult almost. We were not even permitted to go to that either. Only he was allowed to go talk among his friends and fellow religious fanatics.

To get an idea of how long ago my father was born, you need to go back to the presidential term of Rutherford B. Hayes, 1879-1881, the 19th President of the United States.

One year after President Hayes was elected into office, my father Daniel Graham Holcomb was born in Yadkinville, North Carolina, where he was schooled in the Quaker religion and the raising of tobacco.

Yadkin County was filled with farming communities with flue-cured tobacco as the major cash crop. There were seventeen plug tobacco factories in operation in Yadkin County where the county commissioners delayed industrial development of the area by repeatedly not allowing the railroad to construct tracks within the county boundaries until the mid to late 1800's.

During that same year, 1880, Bertha Rutledge, my mother, was born also in Yadkinville, North Carolina. My mother was a descendant of Edward Rutledge who died at the age of thirty-nine, after signing the Declaration of Independence. He was my great-great-great grandfather, if I went back enough greats. His brother, John Rutledge, signed the Bill of Rights and was also a Supreme Court Justice. John must have been a crook somewhere along the line because he was appointed and elevated to Chief Supreme Court Justice. He mysteriously resigned and nobody ever found out why. I think there was probably something in his background that he didn't want exposed. He also served as a Senator and died at the age of forty-nine.

The county and the surrounding area where Graham grew up remained rural for many years of his life.

One year after Graham was born, Thomas Edison invented the incandescent light.

Many memorable and historical events occurred during the years that Graham and Bertha were growing into adulthood.

Most likely the two of them were not aware of the fact that North and South Dakota, Montana, Washington, Idaho, Wyoming, and Utah were admitted to the Union and that the United States of America was growing at a rapid pace.

The massacre at Wounded Knee, South Dakota, occurred but it happened so far away from North Carolina that the news did not arrive until everything was long past over and done with.

President Benjamin Harrison was elected to a term from 1889-1893 followed by the Election of Grover Cleveland, 1893-1897.

A gasoline tractor was built by John Froelich in 1892 and George B. Seldon was granted a U.S. Patent for an automobile in 1895. That was also the year Jack Dempsey was born in Manassa, Colorado.

1896 brought with it Rural Free Delivery allowing the farmers to assign less time to traveling back and forth to town to pick up mail. In that same year, the Spanish American War erupted.

In the mean time, Graham and Bertha, were united in wedlock and in 1898 Lytton, my eldest brother, was born followed in 1900 by the birth of my brother, George.

Two years passed and Laura was born in 1902, with my brother Clifford next in line in 1904.

During that birthing time from 1900 to 1904, President McKinley was shot and Theodore Roosevelt continued his term. The Wright Brothers built their first airplane.

Only bits and pieces of the national news managed to get to Graham and Bertha. It all had to be passed by word of mouth.

1906 brought with it an important part of rural life: "The only thing that can make us give up our radio is poverty. The old radio is the last thing moved out of the house when the sheriff comes in," said Will Rogers.

In 1907, Oklahoma was admitted as a state and the Holcomb family consisting of Graham, Bertha, Lytton, George, Laura, and Clifford left Yadkinville and moved to Virginia where Graham raised corn and peanuts to scratch out a living for his growing family.

Hudson Holcomb was born in 1908 in Sedley, Virginia, around the time that General Electric patents the first electric toaster.

The NAACP (National Association for the Advancement of Colored Peopled) was founded as the National Negro Committee in New York City in 1909.

Baby brother Hudson was two years old in 1910 but his life ended that year when a gate fell on him.

The Holcomb family packed up for a cross country trip to Nebraska to raise wheat. At that time, Jack Dempsey was learning to box as "Kid Blackie" and New Mexico and Arizona became states.

When my sister, Dorothy, was welcomed to Nebraska, President Woodrow Wilson had taken office.

A year later World War I came into being.

That was the same year that Lytton, age 16, left home to strike out on his own.

In 1915, Fred, my brother born in Nebraska near the Platte River, was deaf but he eventually learned sign language although he never, ever spoke aloud.

George left home in 1916 to work in the gold mines in Nevada.

1917 brought with it the declaration of war on Germany, the creation of the Draft, and a move by the Holcomb family back to Virginia.

Brother Byron was born in Sedley, Virginia, 1918, and my father, Graham, bought a plot for family burials in Sedley.

The boys in the family tried to keep up with the escapades of Jack Dempsey. In 1919 Dempsey beat Jess Willard for the heavyweight title and was labeled the "Manassa Mauler" for doing so.

Taylor, the boy who could do no wrong, was born in Sedley in 1919. Other than the birth of Taylor, 1919 was a busy year for historical events.

The Susan B. Anthony Amendment was ratified in thirty six states becoming the 19th Amendment to the Constitution which allows women voting rights. The Panama Canal was completed and movie houses became a common sight in rural areas. The 18th Amendment proclaimed the Prohibition Era and alcohol sales were disallowed.

The Holcomb family packed up again for a cross country trek, this time to Missouri. My sister, Laura, 18, went to work for a telephone company in Cleveland where she married Mr. Diebold, the inventor of a machine that made seamless copper tubing.

CHAPTER 2

1920'S

My father would not permit a doctor in the house. He did not believe in doctors. When I was born, April 2, 1921, there was no doctor present. There was no record ever made of me being born although I was, it is evident I was, because I am alive today.

While New York City was hearing about Professor Albert Einstein's theory of relativity, a mother was giving birth to Stanley E. Holcomb in a log cabin in the Ozark Mountains of Missouri near Long Lane Town.

My mother had no doctor while she was pregnant with me or any of the other children.

1922 brought with it a new birth that being my brother, Earl, who died two weeks later.

We lived on a farm in the Ozark Mountains of Missouri, in a log cabin where I was born. The family stayed on that farm for nearly four years after my birth.

I have only one recollection of living in that log cabin. My memory is of not of the house; I remember nothing of the house, but I do remember a chicken and a barn. The reason for that memory is that something happened that's as clear to me today as it was the day it happened.

We had a chicken that would not lay an egg where the other chickens laid their eggs. That chicken would only lay an egg up in the hay loft of a certain barn. My two older brothers, the ones that were still at home were Byron and Taylor, and I would go out to the barn each day to get the egg.

To get into the attic, hayloft, there were no steps; you had to use a ladder. I could not climb the ladder so my older two brothers climbed up the ladder and Byron put the egg in his pocket. This was the first time he was allowed to bring the egg down the ladder. When he reached the bottom and stepped onto the floor, he had a scrambled egg in his pocket. The next time and each time after that, he would tie a rope around his waist, tie it to a bucket, and climb up that ladder, with Taylor. If they found an egg, they would pull the bucket up, put the egg in the bucket, and gently lower the bucket to the ground.

On one particular day that I remember so well, I wanted so much to go into the hayloft with my brothers. Of course, I was too small and I couldn't go.

My brothers climbed up to the hayloft where they found no egg that day so Taylor pulled the bucket up and took it to the front of the hayloft where he lowered it down to the front door where they put in the hay from the ground. Underneath that front door was where the horses stayed and as they would go into the barn they would drop their manure. The same would happen when they exited the barn so there was plenty of manure. Taylor told me to fill the bucket with manure.

If you don't know what manure looks like, it comes out in clusters about the size of an egg and shaped similar to an egg except that it was very dark. The clusters would dry if they lay in the sun for an hour after they were dropped. You could actually pick one up and put it in your pocket without getting any stain on you.

I filled the bucket with horse biscuits as we used to call them in those days, some people still call them horse biscuits rather than horse manure. Taylor pulled it up, untied the rope from the bucket, and threw the bucket out into the yard.

I would have been all right had I stayed where I was, but I didn't. I started to run right under the bucket and it hit me on the head. It just about scalped me.

My two brothers took me in the house where my mother pulled my scalp back over my skull. She tied a rag around it to hold it in place until it healed.

Until this day, if you feel my head, you can feel a dent in my skull about three inches long where the rim of the bucket hit it and crushed the skull in.

Some people who have known me for a long time and knew what happened to me when I was a young boy, say, "The only thing wrong with Stanley is that when he was little, he got hit on the head with a bucket of horse shit."

In 1925, we moved from the log cabin to a little town called Ivor in Southampton County, Virginia. We rented the property from a man named Brantley and we stayed in the house for one year working the farm.

Southampton County, in 1831, was the location of the most serious slave rebellion in the history of the United States. August 21-22 of the year of the infamous Southampton Insurrection, under the leadership of Nat Turner, a slave, fifty-eight white people were killed along an unknown number of blacks. The legal authorities captured Nat Turner and his followers leading to the trial, conviction, and hanging of twenty of the captives.

My father moved down the road about three-quarters of a mile to another house. There my sister, Nancy, was born.

In neither of those two houses do I remember anything that happened.

Then from there, the next year, he moved us to the other side of Ivor which was about four miles.

I do have a recollection of a few things that happened in that Ivor house.

One, when the corn crop was ready to pick in the fall, it was picked and brought into the yard where it was piled in big piles. The neighbors from all around would come and they'd have what you call a corn shucking. They'd sit there and shuck corn all day and into the night, if necessary, to get the big pile of corn shucked so it could be put in the barn.

We would take some of the shucks and put them into a large sack-like things made out of flour sacks sewn together. Those would be our new mattresses. We were so poor we could not buy mattresses for the beds so we used the shucks. You can imagine what they sound like when you roll over at night.

Second, I wanted a sling shot. I was not big enough to make one. A little colored boy that lived down the road told me he'd make me one for a nickel. Well, I saved my pennies and I was told if I had five pennies that would add up to a nickel. So, I gave him the five pennies and he made me a slingshot.

I was so proud of the slingshot. It was the only thing I'd ever had in my entire life that I'd gotten on my own. I ran into the house and showed it to my father who was standing in the kitchen while my mother was cooking dinner.

"Where did you get that?" demanded my father.

"From the colored boy down the road," I answered.

"How much did you give for it?"

"A nickel."

My father jerked the slingshot from my hand. He lifted the lid off of the wood burning cook stove on which my mother was cooking. I could see the flame from the wood burning in the wood box. My father threw my slingshot into the flames. I could see it starting to catch on fire. I wanted to reach into the flames and pull it back to safety but I couldn't.

My father took me into the other room where he had a two-inch wide, two-foot long leather strap that he kept with which to beat us children.

"You did something on your own without asking my permission to do it," he explained as he beat the living hell out of me.

That was about the last thing I remembered from the place.

In 1928, we moved from Ivor to Suffolk, actually it was about six miles out from Suffolk, to a farm that we rented that was about forty miles from Ivor. This farm was owned by three old maiden ladies. One of the ladies, Suzy Rabey, took a liking to me.

Ringworm appeared on the side of my face and, of course, my father would not do anything for me. The ringworm kept growing and growing and it was about the size of a silver dollar.

"Can I take the boy into town with me?" Suzy Rabey asked my father.

"Yes," answered my father whose only goal was to impress her.

Suzy took me to the drugstore.

"If you permit this druggist to put something on your face that will cure ringworm, I will buy you a new pair of pants," she said as she stood me in front of the druggist.

"Yes, Ma'am," was my answer. I really wanted a new pair of pants. I had never owned a pair of pants or any clothes that were bought in the store. I had only homemade hand-me-downs that my brothers had worn.

When we arrived home my father was in the back yard. I was so proud of my new pants that I went running up to him to show them to him. He immediately noticed my face and the iodine that the druggist had applied to it.

"What happened to your face?" he demanded.

"The druggist put some medicine on it to make it better," I explained worriedly.

"You shouldn't be permitting somebody, anybody to put medicine on your face. That's just plain evil," he screamed at me as he beat the living hell out of me with a stick.

He took my new pants away from me and would never let me wear them again.

He would never let me go anywhere with Suzy again.

The Rabey sisters raised registered turkeys and they sold the eggs for one heck of a price. Suzy would take them to the fair and show the turkeys off every year and get a blue ribbon for them.

Every time I would walk through the yard one old turkey gobbler would come strutting up to me with his wings dragging the ground. They do that to wear off the feathers making the feather quills sharp and stiff. That old turkey gobbler would come up to me, hop up, and slap me in the face with his wing. He would just cut my face something terrible with the sharpened end of the wing. Every time I would have to take the water back to the field and also go back there to hoe the corn, I would have to pass the old turkey gobbler. I was really afraid of that turkey. I wasn't but about eight years old and it was a huge turkey, big gobbler, much bigger than me.

This particular day I decided I had had enough. I got myself a broomstick, one where the broom was worn out leaving mostly stick. I got that stick that was actually the handle. I took it with me. I had it beside me. I was ready. Here comes that turkey strutting up to me; mean old gobbler. It started strutting around me with his wings dragging the ground. He focused his beady black eye on me. I could feel it burning my skin. He fluffed his feathers like a fighter strutting in a ring. He was getting ready to hop up and slap me with his wings.

I took that broom handle and swung it hitting him right on the head.

He fell down. I thought I had killed him. That mean old gobbler flopped and hopped around like a chicken with his head cut off. He couldn't stand up. I had really knocked him for a loop. I thought I had killed him.

I didn't know what I was going to do. I killed a prize turkey. I knew I would get killed just like that turkey. I wouldn't just get a beating I would get killed for doing that.

I stayed there and watched him until he finally got his senses back to where he could keep his balance and not fall over when he got up; then he ran away.

Every time after that I would go through that yard and that old turkey gobbler would see me, he would head for the other direction. He would take off in a big hurry. He remembered that hit on the head. I was so happy that he remembered it.

When I was ten years old I knew how to fix almost anything. This little fact made my father very angry with me.

My father bought a 1923 Dodge in 1933 and paid fifteen dollars for it. He trusted my older brother to work on it but not me. When I told my father what was wrong with the car, he beat me.

From sun-up to sun-down I picked weeds. I had to carry hundred pound bags of fertilizer and corn when I was ten years old.

"Stanley, you will never be able to pay me back for all that you have cost in raising you. You were a mistake. You were never invited into this family. You will never amount to anything in your life," my mother would tell me every time she got the opportunity.

There was never any love.

Then she would tell my father about everything I did that she didn't approve of and I would get a beating.

The Great Depression started in 1929 with the crash of the stock market. The trials and tribulations of the rich did not affect us except for the fall in prices for the farm produce we raised to make enough money to buy the things we couldn't make or grow on the farm.

My brother, George, returned home from Nevada in a Cadillac covered with what had to be $10,000 worth of silver trim. In 1928, $10,000 was worth a lot more than it is nowadays.

George had worked in the gold mines and associated with people like J. Paul Getty and Jack Dempsey. I thought George was really rich.

CHAPTER 3

1930'S

My father and mother were married for sixty nine years but my father never, not once, took my mother out to dinner. He would eat out when he went to sell the vegetables grown on the farm.

I remember when I was ten my father bought me one hamburger that cost him five cents. When I was eleven, my sister took me into town and bought me my first hot dog for three cents.

We had good food on the farm but we weren't allowed to eat it. An example of the good food would be the eggs that we had to sell to make money. They were not for family consumption. Those eggs brought into my daddy's hands the good sum of ten cents a dozen.

Once in a while when one of us was sick, we would get a poached egg for breakfast. Sometimes we would pretend to be sick to get that egg but that was a dangerous trick to play because if we were caught there would be hell to pay.

We raised four hundred hogs to cure but none to eat in the house. We had cows but we weren't allowed to eat the butter. Of course, we had to make that butter but we sold it for twenty-five cents a pound. My father would then buy margarine at ten cents a pound for family consumption. The margarine tasted like butter so we really didn't miss it.

The margarine was white and it looked like rendered lard. There was a little yellow package of plastic that had yellow powder. You would take the yellow powder, put it in the margarine, and mix it up. It looked yellow like butter although you could never get it completely mixed. It had streaks of yellow and white in it.

When they milked the four cows, they would bring in the milk. It was my job to separate milk from the cream. I stood there and cranked that dog-gone separator. We got about eight or nine gallons of milk in the morning and eight or nine gallons of milk at night. I had to stand there, pour the milk into the big bowl at the top, and then crank, crank, crank to separate the cream from the milk. We sold cream and butter. The cream that we made butter out of would go into a churn. It was one that had a crank on it and it was my job to also sit there and crank that thing until we got butter out of it.

The one we had could hold two gallons of milk. It had the paddle that went down in it and then go all the way to the top. The gears were higher and the paddles would turn a lot faster than an ice cream maker. The gears turned that paddle and it was like using your hand in the older churns. It took twenty minutes for each container full. I would do two or three of them a day; so, probably a total of an hour I would have to crank that machine. I would have crank to separate it for at least an hour maybe two hours. It took me an hour in the morning and an hour at night separating the milk from the cream.

Then I would have to take the cream separator apart and wash it really well, dry it, and put it back together so it would be ready for the next churning session either morning or night.

I was nine years old when I first started the churning task. I was twelve when I finished that assigned task and moved on to different chores.

We grew many vegetables like corn, snap beans, black-eyed peas, lima beans, cabbage, cucumbers, lettuce, kale, onions, radishes, sweet potatoes, white potatoes, pumpkins, peppers of all kinds because they were what my daddy liked to eat. We had fruits of all kinds, too; watermelons, cantaloupes, and the like. We sharecroppers got a small portion of the crop that my father sold. The largest part of the crop went to the land owner.

There was a small separate garden for my father to tend to so he could grow enough to feed his family. We were allowed to chop down wood for heating and cooking at no cost.

We were sharecroppers leasing 60-80 acres of land to grow those vegetables and, of course, peanuts. The peanuts were sold in Suffolk for ¾ cent a pound. Mr. Obici, the land owner, inspected the peanuts himself. He owned and operated a small children's zoo and 4H kids from all around the area came visiting. I knew Mr. Obici and he would let me go riding around in his Model-T Ford for the fun of it.

Whenever my father decided to move to another town, that was it—no discussions were allowed.

The neighbor down the road wanted to borrow me to help him plant sweet potatoes.

"Sure, sure," said my father making every effort to impress the neighbor with his good will.

I worked all day gathering sweet potato plants and dropping them about eighteen inches apart where the neighbor would plant them into the ground. It took us the whole day to complete the task.

That night when we went to the house, the neighbor gave me twenty cents. That was the most money I had ever had in my entire life.

I was rich.

The man across the street that owned a little grocery store also had some sweet potatoes to plant.

"Boy, could you come and help me plant my sweet potatoes tomorrow?" he asked me.

Of course, I had to ask my father who was glad to say yes.

We were finished planting sweet potatoes by twelve o'clock. I was so disappointed because I wanted to work all day. I thought he would probably give me twenty cents, too.

We entered his grocery store at noon time where there was fifteen cents laying on the counter. He reached over, picked up the change, and handed it to me.

I now had a total of thirty five cents, fifteen cents from today and twenty cents from the other neighbor.

I was a truly wealthy person.

In the grocery store there was a stalk of bananas hanging from the ceiling. Back then, you didn't buy bananas by the pound, you bought them two for a nickel or three cents apiece or two cents apiece all depending on the size of them. The grocer reached up, pulled one off the stalk, and gave it to me. The first banana I'd ever had in my entire life. I started to eat it with the peeling on it.

"Let me show you how to peel it," he said as he reached toward my banana.

That banana was the best flavored thing I had ever tasted. I savored the sweet, pulpy taste slowly hoping it would last forever.

"I have lots of sweet potato plants leftover. You can have them if you want them to plant," said the grocer.

"Can I plant the sweet potatoes the grocery store man had leftover somewhere here on the farm?" I asked my father.

He thought for a moment.

"There is a little corner of land that is difficult for me to get to tend, you can have that for your sweet potatoes," he said.

I dug up that land with a grubbing hoe. I retrieved the sweet potato plants and placed them delicately into the freshly exposed soil. They grew well and that fall I got a bushel of sweet potatoes off that little corner of land.

"You can get sixty five cents a bushel for those sweet potatoes," said the grocer. "If you keep them until Christmas, you can make a dollar for the bushel."

Well, I wasn't an educated person, but I knew a dollar was more than sixty-five cents. I decided to keep the sweet potatoes.

"You can't keep them in the house," said my father. "You can't keep them in the barn, because they will freeze out there. We need to bury them in a manure pile to keep them from freezing."

That's what we did; we buried them in a manure pile.

In a few days, they sweet potatoes were rotten.

My father seemed very pleased that I had lost my sweet potato crop.

Soon after the loss of the sweet potatoes, a strange thing happened to me. This was truly the strangest thing that had happened to me in my entire life even though many strange things have happened since then.

One night while I was sleeping, I was circumcised.

I was the only person in the room, no doctor came, nobody came in the room, and none of my brothers were ever circumcised. I was the only one. When I woke up in the morning, there was no blood on the sheet, no blood anywhere. I just knew I had lost part of my penis. Why? I didn't know. I really didn't know what had happened. The only thing I really knew was that I had the sorest penis in the county.

Even though I was only eight years old, I had to work in the fields. I would take a hoe, go out to chop the weeds out of the corn and the peanuts.

In addition, it was my duty to carry water to my older brothers and my father who also worked in the fields.

One particular day, my two older brothers and I were working in the field we called the back forty. We were working near Suzy Rabey's house when Taylor wanted a bucket of water so he could have a drink. He told me to go to the Rabey's house and get the water.

Now, I knew it was close to twelve o'clock and though none of us had a watch, I still knew it was near noon. The way we could tell that twelve o'clock came was the Planter's Peanut Plant in Suffolk had a huge whistle that made a tremendous noise when it was blowing. They would blow it at twelve o'clock to let all the employees know it was lunch time. The reason it was so loud was because of a lot of the equipment made a lot of noise and it had to be very loud for the employees to hear it. Even though we lived a long way from Suffolk, we could still hear the whistle.

"Taylor it is almost twelve o'clock. How close to twelve o'clock would it be before I would have to go get that bucket of water?"

"Fifteen minutes to twelve," he said.

I bargained a little and got seventeen minutes. I went to the Rabey's house to fill up the bucket.

"What time is it?" I asked one of the Rabey ladies.

"Quarter to twelve," she responded.

I knew there was a hundred pennies in a dollar. I knew also that twenty five pennies made up a quarter. I figured there were a hundred minutes to an hour. So, twenty five minutes would be a quarter to twelve.

I took the bucket of water out to Taylor who drank it down. I went to get my hoe and started chopping out some weeds. Just as I did, the whistle blew.

Sometime later I learned that an hour only has sixty minutes and quarter of an hour is fifteen minutes. I realized that I had wasted that trip going back to take the bucket of water to the field when I could have been going home for lunch.

I have remembered that mistake for the past eighty years.

Shortly after that, in 1931, we moved to the other side of Suffolk about a mile out of town. When we moved into the house, we discovered that there was a newspaper boy that lived down the road. When a new family moved into the area, he would give them one week of free newspapers in order to try and entice them to subscribe to the newspaper.

My father would not permit a newspaper in the house, or a magazine, or a radio.

"It only has evil on the printed pages or over the airwaves. There is nothing good about any of it," he said loudly.

The delivery boy, about sixteen or seventeen years old, had a Shetland pony that he rode to deliver newspapers to his thirteen customers. The small newspaper cost fifteen cents a week if you didn't take Sunday; because, with the Sunday newspaper it was twenty cents.

The first paper that he delivered to our house was a Sunday paper. My brothers and I were looking at it and I remember three things that were in that newspaper. Andy Gump was in it along with Mutt & Jeff and The Katzenjammer Kids.

As soon as my daddy found out that the newspaper boy left one there and we were looking at it, he grabbed it from us immediately and put it right into the fire in the stove. We couldn't read the words but we were looking at the cartoons. Daddy told that newspaper boy not to leave the newspaper at our house ever again.

Just to show you how smart I was and, oh boy, I was really wasn't very smart in those days; there was a kid down the road at a very little distance from our house. He was just a little bit older than I was. I wanted to go down to his house and look at his paper to see if it had any different funnies in it than the one we had. I thought each newspaper would have its own funny papers in it and the stories in them would all be different even though I couldn't read it. We did not know that all of the newspapers had the same funnies in it for the same day. That's how little we knew about newspapers.

Later we learned that the next door neighbor subscribed to the newspaper so we three brothers could go next door and look at the funny papers he had there.

The older siblings in my family left home at an early age so I rarely got to see and visit with them. When I was eight, I met my older sister, Laura, who had married and moved to Ohio. Laura's soon-to-be husband worked for the Otis Telephone Company in the late 1940's in Tennessee. In the market square, there was a tower with a telephone system. Laura could see he was moving up business-wise and that's when the romance started. Her husband bought crystals that made and operated a radio with a battery with one or two stations and a lot of static. She had married up in life by latching onto a man that would become worth a half million dollars back in the 1920's. They owned a house in Ohio and another house in Miami, Florida. Laura stopped by the house and she was driving a sixteen cylinder Cadillac. She also drove a Studebaker during another visit. They had other cars, too,

While Laura was visiting, her husband paid me and my two brothers five dollars each to haul in the firewood.

We were big time rich.

"It's not possible to make so much money honestly; only crooks make that kind of money," commented my father about the half million dollars.

It was during one of Laura's visit that one of the most exciting experiences of my young life occurred. All of us younger children that were left at home piled into my sister's car and travelled to Virginia Beach where we played in the ocean. The best part of the trip was that I got to sit in the rumble seat of a V16 Cadillac the entire time we were on the road.

People kept telling me we lived in Southampton County, but the only way I knew to describe our location was by the nearest town. We may not have lived in the confines of that town but we were close enough to call it home.

County was a label I could not puzzle out, not then anyway.

There were twenty seven years difference between the age of my oldest brother and my youngest brother. My mother had never seen all of her children at home at one time. The oldest children left home before the younger ones were born.

One morning about four thirty, we had gotten up and my oldest sister had been visiting from Ohio. She and her husband were getting ready to leave to go back to Ohio.

We all knew that three of my other brothers were coming to visit from California but we didn't know whether they would get there that day or a week later.

My sister went ahead and left for Ohio; however, about twenty minutes after she and her husband departed, my three brothers from California walked through the door. That was the closest my mother ever came to seeing all of her children at one time.

My mother, Bertha, had to do all the laundry by hand all those years except for a short time when Lytton had given her a used washing machine for which he paid $7.50. During the Depression, most things were cheap. It was a wringer type machine because that was the only kind they made at that time. You had to hand crank the wringer because it was not electric but it was fastened to the washing machine and it was powered by electricity. One person would crank while another person would feed the clothes in it.

You could buy, at that time, rubber buttons for the people who had washing machines because you could run those rubber buttons through the wringer and they wouldn't break. The rubber would flatten down and feed through the wringer without any button destruction. In the early 1930's a lot of the buttons were made out of seashells and they were very brittle.

Ironing was another task performed by my mother. You would heat the little solid irons on the woodstove. The irons had two kinds of handles. One had a steel handle that had to have a piece of cloth wrapped around it otherwise you would burn the heck out of your hand. The other one had a wooden handle in an arch like that you clip onto the iron. Those irons were pointed at both ends but the steel one was pointed at one end and square at the back.

We grew a lot of vegetables at this place; it was only about a mile from Suffolk.

On Saturday morning we would take a lot of the vegetables into town, peddle them door-to-door and make a little money at it.

We also raised about two to four hundred hogs. Instead of selling them for two and one half cents a pound, that was the price then for a live hog, we slaughtered the hogs. We cured them and received ten cents a pound for the sides, ten cents a pound for the sausage, fifteen cents a pound for the shoulders, and twenty five cents for the hams. We made quite a bit of money out of doing it that way. It was extra work, but worth it.

I stayed hid as much as I could on Sunday so my mother and father wouldn't know where I was. I didn't want them to find a chore for me to do or find some reason to beat the hell out of me.

My mother was a good cook for what she had to cook. Actually we lived off of mostly vegetables and sometimes a little bit of pork, fat back, and the cheaper parts of the pig. For breakfast we would have milk gravy and potatoes, sometimes flapjacks. We did have syrup to go with it that was homemade. I would take water and put some vanilla flavoring in it along with some sugar. It wasn't too bad a maple tasting syrup for the hot cakes. Then we also had some sugar to put on the hot cakes. I don't know why we put the sugar on there. Today I just put maple syrup on mine.

The only time we ever got to eat an egg it was because one of us was sick and then we would get a poached egg. I pretended to be sick so I could get an egg. I can remember pretending two or three times and I got away with it. I never got caught but I was afraid to do it anymore. I was afraid I would get the hell beat out of me. If my daddy sold the eggs to the grocery store we received ten cents a dozen but if we took it out in trade we got twelve cents a dozen.

My mother made jam out of blackberries or we would pick her some scuppernongs or sometimes she would make apple jelly. Well, if you spread that jam or jelly on a piece of bread it was a fantastic treat. We were fed practically no sweets at all—no candy. I would sneak in the pantry where the food was kept to get a slice of bread and spread some jelly on it when I knew my mother was in another part of the house. I would get out of there quick before I got caught. Dan and I were in the pantry one day and, of course, we got caught. Why I didn't get a beating for it I don't know but we were warned that if we were caught ever again we were going to get beat. Maybe it was a week later, Dan and I sneaked in there, again. We were putting some jam or jelly on the bread and I heard my mother coming. She could hardly walk and she had to have a help her cane to walk. I took off running and I got out of there before she arrived at the pantry. Dan didn't run. He stayed in there. My mother heard him in there. She was trying to get in the pantry to see who was in there but Dan was holding the door.

"Let go of that door," my mother yelled at Dan.

"No—don't come in yet," he answered frantically.

"Why?"

"You have to wait until I put the jam away so I can't get caught," he explained.

She didn't beat him because he was only about five years old. Instead, she explained to him what was meant by getting caught. Well, it was true that she didn't actually catch him eating the sweet treat because he held the door and didn't let her inside the pantry.

After I reached the age of twelve years, Taylor and I had to saw wood. There were a lot of pine trees on the farm at Ivor. My daddy sold the pine wood for $3.50 a cord. We would take logs and saw them four feet long; stack them four feet high, eight feet long to make a cord. Taylor and I got seventy-five cents a cord for sawing and stacking it. That equaled out to thirty-seven and a half cents for each of us. The two of us could saw about two cords a day and we had to make braces so the stacked wood would stand and not fall down. That was a lot of wood to cut. In order to saw the cords, we had to cut the trees down, trim the limbs off of them, take a cross-cut saw to cut them up, and then stack them.

Of course, we had to cut fire wood for the house for winter for heat and to cook meals with the whole year around. We received no payment for that.

Down the road a neighbor wanted me to pick some of his string beans. I helped him pick his string beans and all the while I was watching his guineas. I had always wanted some guineas. I thought they were pretty and made a nice noise when they squalled. He gave me a setting of eggs. A setting is sixteen eggs.

"Father, can I have a chicken that is setting and doesn't have any eggs to set on to hatch so she can hatch the little guineas for me."

"Yes," was my father's short reply.

The hen watched and sat on her eggs diligently.

"Take'em away from the mother," said my father. "I want to put the hen back in the coop so she will quit setting and start laying eggs again. Put the guineas in the corn crib. They'll be fine and safe in the corncrib."

A corn crib is a very open building so air can circulate through the corn and prevent the corn from molding. That same night when I put the guineas in the corn crib, the air turned extremely cold. The little guineas froze to death and I lost every one of them. They all died and I think my father was very happy that they did.

We lived on a farm where the Confederate soldiers had camped. I could go out there after every rain and pick up a hand full of old Civil War musket balls. There had been a lot of Indians in the area so I found many arrow heads in that same field. People would come by buying those musket balls or bullets and arrow heads. They would pay me a penny for each of the old treasures.

After we lived near Suffolk for about a year, the Raeford family moved to Suffolk. They were a family that my father had known in Sedley; a little town about fifty miles from Suffolk.

My father lived in Virginia before he moved to Missouri where I was born.

Mr. Raeford came out to see us and he had a boy about the same age as I was.

"Daniel, could your boy come into town next Sunday to play with my boy?" asked Mr. Raeford.

"Yes," answered my father much to my surprise. The Sedley house was about a mile away from where we lived.

I went to play with the Raeford boy on Sunday.

"I'm thirsty," I said after I looked and looked for a well to get me a cool drink of water. "Can I have a drink of water?"

"Oh, sure," he said as he walked over to the side of the house. There was a thing sticking out of the house that had a handle on it. He took a cup that was hanging on a nail on the outside wall of the house, placed the cup under the thing that was sticking out of the wall, and then he moved the handle. The water came rushing out of the thing and filled the cup.

"Here you go," he said as he handed me the cup that had mysteriously filled with water.

As I was drinking it had come to mind that I had never seen anything like the water coming out of that thing in my entire life. The water tasted really good and it was the most wonderful thing I had ever seen, I mean that water coming out of the thing in the wall.

When I arrived home I couldn't wait to tell my daddy what I had seen.

"Daddy, they had this thing sticking out of the side of the house and fresh, good, clean, clear water came pouring out of it. They didn't have to take a bucket to the well, let it down, and draw the water out. That's what we need. Get one of those things that stick out of the house that the Raeford boy said was called a spigot, put it on the side of the house, turn the handle on the spigot, and the water would come right out. He said that's all you have to do," I explained excitedly

We didn't get a spigot.

On this farm we raised mostly corn and peanuts. We raised a little bit of cotton, some watermelons, but mostly corn and peanuts.

We plowed in the spring and during the summer we would cultivate the field with mules. We would get the weeds out of the fields by taking a hoe and walking down the rows chopping the fresh shoots of green. In the fall, we would pick the corn by hand off the stalk one ear at a time, throw it on the wagon, haul it to the barn, throw the corn off the wagon into the barn, and go back for another load. We could probably get two loads completed in a day having to do it all by hand.

When it was raining or in the winter time when it was too cold or wet to do anything else, we would go the barn and shuck the corn by hand and pile it over in a huge pile. We would shell part of it with a hand-turned sheller. The rest we would save on the cob to feed the mules because they were able to eat it off of the cob.

I never will forget this. I was about ten years old when we were raising peanuts, our main crop. We would save back some of those peanuts and shell them for the seed to plant next growing season. My mother was in the kitchen and she had a big pan of them in her lap. She was shelling them so I decided I was going to help her. I get down in front of her where I could reach into the pan getting the peanuts and shelling them. She swung her arm around and popped me upside the head with her hand as hard as she could without spilling the peanuts. I mean she really hit me.

"Why did you do that?" I asked.

"You have an impotent look on your face," she hissed at me.

There was no reason at all to hit me like that and I never did know what she meant by "impotent look."

When we worked the peanuts we would dig them out with a plow and the mules. It took about fifteen people working hard and long hours to dig up the peanuts. We would take a pitch fork, load it up, shake the dirt out of the peanuts, and place them into small piles. We would take slender poles, drive them into the ground, and stack the peanuts on them to dry. We would leave them three weeks to a month until they were completely dry.

A neighbor was hired along with his tractor and a peanut picker to come to our place to pick the peanuts. Once again, about fifteen people were needed to haul the peanuts from the stacks in the field back to the peanut picker. A small group of people would put the peanuts in the picker, another group would take them from the picker and shake them into a basket. From there the peanuts would be poured into a bag. They would sew up the bag that weighed about a hundred pounds when it was full and haul it into the barn. When all the peanuts were picked, we would haul them into town and sell them.

When the peanut picker was sorting out the peanuts to be sold, it would drop the vines out of the backside of the picker. We had to stack those vines in a huge stack. During the winters, we would go get wagonloads of vines at a time and take them into the barn to feed them to the mules and the cow. All of his had to be done by hand.

None of us had a watch although we did have a clock at the house. We had a huge bell that would be rung at twelve o'clock so we would all go in for what we called dinner.

We didn't have to worry about getting to work at the right time each morning because when the sun came up enough for us to go to work, that's exactly what we did. Quitting time and going to supper wasn't a problem either because we worked until dark. Then, and only then, it was time to quit.

On one of the treks into the peanut patch picking peanuts and moving vines, I was working with a young black boy who decided my barefoot made a perfect place to ram his pitchfork.

I don't know if it was an accident or not. All I know is that it hurt. When the pitchfork was yanked out of my foot and the bleeding was stopped, my father saw no reason to take me to procure the services of a doctor to stop any infection. Since the blood flow was halted, there was no need for the expense of a doctor.

The pitchfork went down into the ground and my foot was right there. One of the prongs stuck all the way through my big toe. That toe swelled up huge. A couple of people looked at it a few days later and said that gangrene was setting in and it would kill me or I would have to have my foot taken off if my daddy didn't take me to the doctor and have the infection taken care of. My daddy wouldn't take me.

This happened in 1934 and I guess my guardian angel made me well. My daddy would let me die before he would have taken me to the doctor. I had to hop around and do my work. A sore toe was no excuse not to work.

Also in 1934, my next to the eldest sister decided to leave home to marry a man from Portsmouth, Virginia. My brother, Bryan age 16, decided he was going to Chicago to find a life.

Seemed to me that sixteen was the age when we children were no longer a member of our own family.

Nothing else happened on the Suffolk farm that stayed in my memory except for the day I was out in the barn when a thunderstorm came up. I was holding some old curling irons that I found under the house and lightning struck them. It was a very light strike, it didn't kill me, of course, because if it did I wouldn't be here today. The fact that I'm writing and telling you these stories proves that I didn't die. It did burn some of the skin off of my hand.

We also had cows, four to be exact, on that farm from which we sold the milk. We sold the milk, cream, butter and what have you.

The only money I could make was from a big scuppernong vine that is a kind of grape grown only in the south. In the summer time I would go pick those scuppernongs. I would put them in bags and then take them to a little camp down the road a ways where the Union Camp, a logging company, had a camp where they kept their loggers. I would sell the scuppernongs to the loggers for ten cents a quart. I could pick maybe two or three quarts a day and I thought I was getting rich.

With the money we had saved from growing vegetables in the garden, curing the meat, and selling it, we had saved enough money to buy a farm near Ivor again.

This farm sold for $1,750.00 and it had a nice home on it. There were a hundred and eighty acres of good fertile land. Today that farm would be worth about five hundred thousand dollars. That's the difference in the price of 1933 during the time of Franklin D. Roosevelt and today.

About a year later, my folks sent me into town to pick up something after we finished working in the fields that day. It was dark and I was coming home. Down the road was a graveyard. There were always tales of ghosts coming out of the graveyard and scaring people half to death.

As I was getting ready to walk passed the silent graves, a ghost came up beside me and took hold of my arm. I was so frightened I couldn't move. I don't know how long it was before I was able to start walking again. Finally, I was walking and I could feel the ghost still holding my arm. I could hear him walking beside me.

Down a little further along the road was Peacock Swamp. It had a wooden bridge across it and as anybody knows, because it is a wooden bridge when you walk on it, the boards will rattle. I could hear this ghost rattling on the boards as he walked. I walked on down the road a little ways where there was another road that turned off to the right. That was the road we lived on so I turned there. The ghost still held me by the arm, walking beside me. I could hear him walking, hear him making the noise in the gravel on the road.

Down about a quarter of a mile further was the lane going to our house that was set about a thousand feet back off from the road in a field. You could see the lights burning bright. We continued to walk while the ghost was holding my arm. When we reached our destination the ghost turned me loose after which he turned around and went back into the direction from where we had come. I stood there and listened until he completely got out of hearing distance.

I entered the house and saw that everybody had already eaten dinner. I placed a small amount of food on my plate, but I wasn't able to eat much because I was still awful shook up.

One morning I woke up and was so sick that I stayed in bed all that day and all that night. The next morning my brother Taylor came into the room. Taylor was the one child that mother and father thought the sun rose and set in because there was nothing he could do wrong regardless of what it was. If Taylor stole, cheated, lied he did nothing wrong because he could do no wrong. He was a perfect angel. He was the one that was a little older than me and he also was the one that hit me on the head with a bucket of horse manure.

"Let me see your old coins," demanded Taylor.

I can't remember where I got those old coins but I had placed them in a metal box for safe keeping. I didn't lock the box because it wouldn't have done any good. All you had to do was pick up the box and walk away with it. I locked it anyway and I had four one dollar bills in the box with the old coins.

"Go away," I said weakly.

"I want to see the coins," he whispered harshly.

"I'm too sick to get them, Taylor."

"Where are they?"

"Over there in that metal box."

"It's locked. Give me the key."

"Okay, the key is on the wall behind that table. Get the key and bring the box here and I'll open it for you."

I opened the box. He picked up the coins, looked at them, and put them back.

"That's all I wanted to see," he said as he walked out of the room. When he walked out of the room into the hallway, I couldn't see where he went after he left my room.

During the night, I had what I guess you would call a vision, or whatever, where I saw Taylor reach his hand in that box and take out a dollar bill. I had four dollar bills in the box and one of them was brand new. I actually saw him take the brand new dollar out of the box and stick it into his pocket. When he walked out of the room, I saw him go down the hallway and go up the stairway to the second floor. He entered the room that we only used for guests. In that room against the wall was a vanity that had two drawers on each side of the mirror. Taylor reached for the top drawer on the right-hand side, pulled it out, put the new dollar bill into it, closed the drawer, and walked out of the room.

The next morning I knew that that's what had happened because I could see it as plain as if I had been following him right up the steps and had watched him do it. Very clear, it was all so very clear.

When I was able to get out of bed, I retrieved my locked metal box and sure enough my brand new dollar bill was gone. I walked up the steps, walked over to the vanity, and pulled out the top right-hand drawer. The only thing I could see inside the drawer was a white handkerchief and beneath it was one brand new dollar bill.

"Taylor, I saw you take my dollar bill," I whispered when he entered my room.

"No, you didn't. You were asleep."

"So you admit you took it?"

"Yeah, but you didn't see me."

When I told my mother and father about my vision and having found the dollar bill just as my vision had showed me, they said I was only lying trying to get Taylor in trouble because he didn't do it. He wouldn't do such a thing.

When Taylor was sixteen, I was fourteen at the time, he stole my mother's wedding ring and hocked it at a pawn shop for fifty cents before leaving home. But remember—Taylor could do no wrong.

During this period of time Byron came home from Chicago for a visit. He was driving a car that I really liked and he promised to let me drive it.

When I went to bed that night, I was dreaming about driving Byron's car.

When I awoke, I was sitting behind the steering wheel and the car was purring beneath me like a contented kitten. I don't remember climbing into the car, nor do I remember going anywhere in particular. I woke up driving like it was an ordinary part of my life.

Taylor got a job working for a tire company where he sold tires and pocketed the money. Again, he could do no wrong.

In 1935 Social Security was created to provide retirement insurance, but that didn't matter one bit to me, not at that time.

At the age of fourteen, I sneaked in a theater in Suffolk where I saw my first moving picture, "Buck Jones." It was a B Western. One of many made by the actor called Buck Jones which was only one of his many screen names.

The thrill of sneaking into the picture show was exhilarating, but the marvel of watching the moving picture was out of this world.

Fourteen years old was a good year for me because I met my first sweetheart, Elsie Phelps, age 12. I will always remember Elsie Phelps.

Taylor kept on scheming and getting by with it.

When Taylor was twelve years old and when my older brother that was living at home had reached the age of twelve, my father gave each one of them two acres of land to farm. They could plant whatever they wanted on the land and whatever money was gained when they sold their crop from their land was their money to keep.

He wouldn't do the same for me until I reached the age of fourteen. Before finally getting my land I had to keep reminding him that I had reached and passed the age of twelve and that I wanted my own land to farm just like my brothers.

With my two acres, I planted cotton. Why I planted cotton, I don't know, but it was the largest cotton you had ever seen. It grew as high as a man's head and was completely loaded with cotton. I earned about seventy-eight dollars for the cotton above what it cost me to pay for my fertilizer and seed.

Taylor planted his two acres with peanuts. He earned about the same thing that I did, but he had spent all of it except fifteen dollars. It had been Taylor's plan to buy a Model A from a dealer for ninety dollars. He wanted to borrow seventy-five dollars from me to put with his fifteen so he could get the car.

"I'll give you the crop next year that I plant on the land that daddy gave me to use up to seventy-five dollars," he pleaded with me.

"The only way I would do such a thing is to ask our father to hold back seventy-five dollars, give it to me, and give you whatever is left over," I said knowing full well that Taylor couldn't be trusted.

My father agreed.

Anything that belonged to my father you did not touch, nothing, but there was one thing he did do for me. He had a double barrel hammer shotgun that he would let me use to go hunting. I guess the only reason he allowed me to use the shotgun was that I would come home with some rabbits or a squirrel or two. I loved to hunt. I was about fourteen when I started supplying the family with the fresh game. If we didn't eat the game the neighbors would buy them from me for ten cents per squirrel and a quarter each for the rabbits.

I had an uncle whom I had never seen before come from Iowa. He went to my father and did the same deal that I had done. That fall, when the peanuts were harvested and sold, my daddy took my money I had loaned to Taylor and gave my seventy-five dollars to my uncle and there was a dollar and change left over that he gave to me. That's all I ever received of that money except one time later my brother did give me five dollars on it. To this day, I have not received one single penny of that money other than those five dollars.

My father would not let me, my two older brothers, my younger brother, and my younger sister go to school. For some reason, he got it in his head that it was an evil place. If you went to school, all you were taught was evil. So, I had never been to school at all a day in my life.

We were kept so ignorant that I did not know what Christmas was. I did not know about Easter, the Fourth of July, or Thanksgiving. It was just another day that I did not hear mention of in the house. If I would hear somebody talk about it, any holiday, I would ask about it.

"That's just something evil. You shouldn't talk about it. Don't even remember that you heard about it," he would say in complete and total earnest.

You can imagine how ignorant I was.

One day the sheriff stops by with a warrant for my father for not sending us to school.

It seems there was a law in Virginia. It had been in existence for several years stating that you had to send you children to school until they were fifteen years old. My father had gotten away with breaking the law for several years.

"You can either send your three youngest children to school since all of your other children are older than fifteen or I can serve the warrant and take you to jail," explained the Sheriff.

You can bet your bottom dollar we went to school.

When I was about fourteen, I got a bike. It was a used one and it was a girl's bicycle. My daddy bought it for me. I don't know why he bought me a girls bicycle. Byron and Taylor got boys bicycles. I was ashamed to ride a girls bicycle because they would call me a sissy. I did ride it but where people could not see me. Down the road about a quarter of mile was where a dentist lived and he had a daughter, the only child he had, about my age. She was nice looking and I wanted to get to know her better.

I did venture to ride the bicycle down to her house quite often and sometimes she would be out in the yard. In front of her house there was a slight little downhill where the bicycle would just roll if you didn't peddle it and it would keep on going. I didn't have any shoes meaning I was barefooted and I was acting smart wanting her to notice me. I took my feet off of the pedals and the bike kept on rolling because it was downhill. I was sticking my foot out in front and I stuck it right in the spokes of the front wheel. I broke out about three spokes with my foot stuck in there barefooted. Boy oh boy, did that hurt. Of course, I fell down and embarrassed myself while she was watching me. I was trying so hard to show off.

I didn't break my foot but it sure was sore. It wouldn't have made any difference if I did break my foot, my daddy would not have taken me to the doctor.

When I was fourteen years old my second oldest brother, Byron, was at home. He had an old 1923 Dodge automobile for which he paid fifteen dollars. He had been gone somewhere and he was returning home at about eleven o'clock.

In my sleep I got up, walked outside, and climbed into the car. I hadn't ever driven a car for more than thirty minutes prior into climbing Byron's car, if I drove it that much. I drove into the town of Ivor. I went to sleep. I was sleepwalking.

I drove into town where I was parked on the side of the road waiting for my brother so he wouldn't have to walk the two miles at that time of night to get home after he got back from Suffolk. I was there waiting for him to take him home or let him drive the car home. I went to sleep again. He didn't show up and I went to sleep in the car again.

About one o'clock in the morning Bud Brian, they called him Little Bud, saw me. He was a fellow that I knew there in town who lived directly across from the school house. He said I was sitting there in the car about three quarters of a mile from the school house.

"Stanley, can you give me lift the rest of the way home?" he asked me.

"Yeah, sure, climb in," he said I told him.

He got into the car and it was pitch dark because there was no full moon.

A few days later when he saw me again he said, "You were acting crazy. You wouldn't turn the lights on in the car. I would turn them on and you would turn them off. It was so dark I couldn't see where we were going."

I remembered the next day what I had done. I could see plainly that it was dark but I could see. I had no problem with trying to see at the school house which was right across the street from where he lived. The school house was fenced in and there was one little narrow gate just wide enough to drive through. It was open so I drove through there in pitch dark. Bud couldn't see the fence at all or the gate because it was so dark but I had no trouble seeing it. I drove through and he told me he was never so glad to get out of a car in his life. There were trees in the school yard and I circled around through the trees back out onto the street. I stopped the car and let him out to go into his house.

"You scared the living daylights out of me," he whispered harshly.

I went back uptown and I waited until about three o'clock and Byron still hadn't shown up so I drove back home. I still never woke up until it was time to get out of bed to go to work doing my daily chores.

I did sleep walk quite a bit after that but that was the only time I drove a car so many miles in my sleep. I drove the car one time after that but I had just started out of the yard when I woke up. I can't remember why I was driving the car that time. I don't recall ever doing it again.

I lacked five months of being fifteen years old so I went to school those five months and that is the limit of the formal education that I have.

That year I decided to plant cotton again on my two acres.

The time we got off from chores around the farm, was Saturday afternoon. The Friday before the Saturday that I was going to plant the cotton, there came a tremendous downpour and the land was muddy. I wanted to wait until the next Saturday.

"No, you're going to plant it today or I'm not going to let you have the mules to plant it with," said my father.

My uncle agreed to help me with it so he took one mule and laid the rows off. I followed him with the fertilizer sewer, sewing the fertilizer into the row.

It was so wet in some places that the mules would mire to the belly. We would have to unhook them, move them down to a drier spot, pull the fertilizer sewer down, hook them back up, and go on. Just as we were finishing with the fertilizer sewer, a neighbor came up and wanted to borrow the cotton planter.

My father loaned it to him.

The neighbor came by where I was finishing up with fertilizer sewing and waved at me as he went by with the cotton planter.

"Why?" I asked my father.

"You said you didn't want to plant today anyway so I told him to go ahead and take it," answered my father with a smirk.

The neighbor didn't bring the borrowed cotton planter back.

That weekend another tremendous down pour hit that washed all of the fertilizer out of the rows that I had sewed. The fertilizer wasn't covered over because the cotton hadn't been planted.

The next weekend he still hadn't returned the cotton planter so I went down to see him and find out why.

"Well, Boy, your father told me he wasn't going to plant any cotton. He didn't need the cotton planter so I could keep it as long as I wanted it."

I told him my story.

"I'll bring it back right now, immediately."

He did as he said.

I planted the cotton.

It didn't bare anything at all hardly because the fertilizer had been all washed out and the land it was planted on was not as good as the other land I had used. After I paid for my fertilizer and seeds, I made about two dollars, not over three dollars I'm sure.

Right after I picked my cotton my father decided that he was going to sell the farm to my Uncle Elwood and move to Winston-Salem, North Carolina.

I lacked a few months being sixteen years old at that time but he told me that he was not going to take me with the family. I would be on my own.

I got a little bit of work pulling weeds for Mr. Sadler who lived down the road a piece. I worked for twelve hours each of five days and I earned a total of $5.25 travelling money.

I packed the few clothes I had, whatever I had. I hitchhiked down to Portsmouth where my sister lived. I stayed with her a few days. She told me about an aunt that I had in Yadkinville, North Carolina, which was about twenty miles outside of Winston-Salem.

I didn't know I had this aunt until my sister told me. I was not ever permitted to know that I had any grandmothers, grandfathers, aunts, uncles, cousins, or any other relatives. I never met any of them until my uncle came from Iowa just before I left the farm.

I decided to hitchhike to Yadkinville, North Carolina, which I did.

I found my aunt and she said she was glad to see me. I told her my story and, of course, she wanted to help me very much.

She took the Winston-Salem newspaper and each morning she would look through the classifieds for a job for me hoping that I could find one where I could go to work and accomplish something.

There were few jobs during the depression. However, after about three weeks, I found a job with a firm selling magazines that had a traveling crew that was going from North Carolina down to Florida to Texas, Missouri, and then back to Chicago to headquarters.

There were about ten people in the crew and we all packed into two automobiles. Each driver would load the car, take us out in the country just about as far as they thought we could walk back into town by night. We would walk back in and as we walked by the farm houses, we would stop and try to sell magazines. We would sell a few, just barely enough to make a living.

We would go into small towns and there would be small hotels, little frame hotels where we would make a deal with the owner. We would rent one room with two double beds where four of us would stay in the room, two to a bed. We would usually get the room for about eight dollars a week, sometimes six dollars, other times we would have to pay ten dollars. If we paid eight dollars and there were four of us in the room that meant it would cost each of us two dollars per week which was about as much as we could afford.

The best I can remember is that we would make about twenty cents or maybe as much as a dollar and a quarter for selling a magazine subscription. It would average to about sixty cents. If we made sixty cents a day to a dollar a day, we weren't doing too badly. We could survive on that. Sometimes we would make as much as ten dollars a week, in an extremely good week, that is.

We would walk down the road stopping at each house trying to sell the magazine, getting closer and closer to the pickup point by nightfall. If we were at the pickup point early, we would wait for the guy to come and pick us up. If not, we would continue walking down the road and he would drive down the road in the direction from which we were coming until he met us to pick us up and take us back to town.

By Christmas we had arrived in Atlanta where we were in a small hotel that had a world globe in the lobby. I didn't know what a globe was. I was looking at it and I didn't want to let the other boys know that I was as stupid as I was.

"I bet you don't know what that thing is," I said to one of the boys so he could tell me about what I looking at and I wouldn't seem so ignorant.

"Yes, I do. It's a globe." he answered.

"Well, I bet you don't know what those things are that are drawn on it," I said as I continued to probe for an answer.

"I do so. They are countries," he answered defensively.

"Yes, well then do you know where we are on there if that's what it is?" I continued.

"Of course, I do," he answered as he put his finger on Atlanta.

"Boy, that's a little dot down there that says Atlanta."

I figured from Atlanta that I had been all over the entire world because I had come from Virginia, a little town called Ivor, down to Winston-Salem, North Carolina, through South Carolina and part of Georgia. My goodness, that had to be at least three-quarters of the world.

"I bet you can't show me where we started at in Winston-Salem," I challenged.

He put his finger on Winston-Salem and I looked at it. My gosh, that's only about a half an inch or an inch from Winston-Salem to Atlanta.

I looked at the rest of the globe and to my surprise I haven't been anywhere. I have even hardly been out of my back yard.

Right then I realized I was very dumb. I knew nothing and it was time I really started to try to learn something.

From Atlanta, we traveled on through the country, down through all of Georgia, down to Florida across Alabama, Louisiana, Texas, then on up through Arkansas, part of Oklahoma on up to Chicago.

At that point, I quit. I had just a few dollars. I didn't have enough money to buy a bus ticket back to Winston-Salem so I started hitchhiking.

I had gotten back to West Virginia and I was riding with a fellow who was not going to the next big town. It was already dark, very cloudy, and it started drizzling rain. He let me out in the country in the mountains, and I went walking down the road. I could hardly stay on the road because there was no moonlight to see. I was wet from the drizzling rain and so very miserable.

As I was walking down the side of the mountain I saw a light and I knew there had to be a house there. It wasn't too far off the road. I finally found the path that led to the house. I knocked on the door of what was only a one room shack. My knock was answered by an elderly man with his wife standing to the side.

I told him my story.

"I am hungry and would like to have something to eat. I can pay you a few pennies for the food," I said.

"I won't take your money, Young Man, but I will share what little food we have with you," said the elderly man with his wife nodding her head in agreement.

The elderly man and his wife were very poor and all they had was some fatback and cornbread.

The wife warmed the food up on a wood cook stove.

"Eat all of it you want," she instructed.

I ate enough to keep me from being hungry.

"I'm sorry I can't let you spend the night here. We have only one room and one bed," said the elderly man apologetically.

"I understand, Sir," I said as I left the small one room shack.

It had stopped drizzling rain and I walked back out to the road. I kept going down the road, maybe a mile to so, until I came to a railroad crossing.

The moon came out, just for a split second and when it did, I saw a little shack that was beside the railroad track on the right, just a few feet off from the road. I almost got there before the moon went back under the clouds, but I found my way to it anyway, and found an unlocked door. I went inside, felt around the room, and the only thing in there was a bench next to one of the walls. I stretched out on that bench and finally went to sleep.

Sometime during the night I woke up. There was a light shining through the window and an awful noise. I was so frightened I didn't know what to do. I really didn't know where I was, waking up like that from my sleep in a strange place; but, then I realized that I was in the little shack by the railroad track.

I looked out the window and the train was coming directly toward the shack. To me, it looked like it was going to run right through the shack. At about that time, the train got to the shack and, of course, it passed just a few feet away. It really frightened me half to death.

After the train passed, I lay back down on the bench and tried to go back to sleep. I don't think I slept more than thirty minutes the rest of the night because I was so shook up.

The next morning the sun came out and I started hitchhiking again. I hitchhiked back to Winston-Salem. I found out where my parents had moved to and I went to see them. My parents told me that my oldest brother had moved to High Point, North Carolina, and was working for Hoover Vacuum Cleaner Company.

I hitchhiked up to High Point, North Carolina, which was only about twenty more miles and I went to see my brother.

It is 1937 and I am sixteen years old.

"I'm going to start rebuilding vacuum cleaners as well as selling new ones for Hoover. I could really use the help," my brother told me upon my arrival. "What I do is go to Greensboro, North Carolina, and buy old vacuum cleaners that have been traded in for the new Electrolux. The Electrolux is really selling well, now, and the sales should be pretty hot.

"I will buy those vacuum cleaners for fifty cents to not over two dollars and a half a piece. The condition that they are in tells me what price to pay. I buy new replacement parts and a lot of those parts come out of Canada. For the Hoover brand, I would get a bag with a great big H on it. It wouldn't say Hoover, because it couldn't. For the other ones, I would get bags that match. I will get wheels for them, new electric cords, new plugs, and spray paint the metal parts to make it look like brand new.

"For the ones that are aluminum, so many of the parts were made out of that now-a-days, I have an electric buffing wheel with buffing compound."

"Show me how to do the buffing," I said because I was willing to learn to pay my way.

I would buff the aluminum until it looked just like a mirror. I mean to tell you it looked brand new. You put new wheels on it, a new bag, paint the handle black, a new cord, and it looked like a brand new vacuum cleaner.

I would sell the vacuum cleaners for a dollar down and fifty cents a week. I would sell them for ten dollars and the most I would get for the betters ones would be fifteen dollars.

My brother gave me half of the profit for selling them and he didn't charge me any room and board. I did all right for about six months and then my brother had to leave because he went to work for Sears Roebuck in Danville.

Fortunately, I found a job in a hosiery mill the same day he left and I stayed there six months until I was laid off.

I hitchhiked back to my parents' house which was six miles out of Winston-Salem, North Carolina. My mother, Bertha, and my father, Graham, didn't have a telephone, radio, or newspaper in the house. I was unable to communicate with them to let them know I was coming home. I didn't know what the reception would be like.

When I arrived, it so happened that it was time to cut up a lot of wood for the winter to heat the house and to cook. My father needed somebody to help cut it with a cross cut saw because the task required a man on each end of the saw. For two weeks we cut wood.

At about four o'clock in the afternoon my father took me aside and said. "Your mother and I had a talk and we decided that we raised you long enough. You'll have to go."

"Do you want me to leave this afternoon?" I asked.

"No, you can wait until morning," he replied.

I guess the two weeks of hard labor was enough to pay for my room and board. Now that the hard labor has come to an end, I was no longer needed or wanted.

I walked to the mail box and was pleasantly surprised to find a card written to me from the hosiery mill at High Point asking me to return to work immediately. The timing couldn't have been more appreciated.

I earned twenty-five cents an hour working three days a week. Sometimes I would get to work a fourth day which would give me either six or eight dollars for a week's work. Out of the money would come six or eight cents for Social Security leaving me five dollars and ninety-four cents or seven dollars and ninety-two cents. I paid five dollars a week for room and board so I would have at least ninety-four cents left per week.

I saw an ad in the newspaper in a little store downtown that said a man wanted somebody to help him work at the store on Saturdays. I applied for the job and Adolf Herman gave it to me.

As I worked with Adolf he told me some of his background and his reason for being the man he was.

Adolf Herman was born in 1875 into a poor family. He grew up amid the hatred for Jews. His parents lived in a dirt floor hut but they wanted him to have a better life. He heard of ships sailing from the Balkans to America so he was determined to hitch a ride aboard one the seaworthy vessels.

With little food and only the clothes on his back, he walked to the docks. At two o'clock in the morning, he sneaked aboard.

After his food ran out, he sneaked into the galleys and stole enough food to keep himself going until the crew noticed the missing food items. They waited in the darkness for him to make an appearance and when he did, they snatched him up and took him to the captain. A stow-away stealing food is a serious crime for which he could have been thrown overboard but the captain felt sorry for him and let him live. Adolf became the captain's boy until the ship docked in Argentina and then he discovered to his dismay that he had sailed to the wrong America. He wanted to go to North America, not South America. The living conditions in South America were not much better than Russia with one exception, it was warmer.

Adolf had no choice but to reach North America by whatever means possible. He begged for food and slept in the woods where the Indians lived. He spoke no Spanish or any other language that they could understand. Half way through his journey, the Indians captured him. He managed to get free and ran away towards what is now the Suez Canal which was another obstacle because he had to get across that body of water. Some kind-hearted fishermen let him board their vessel to cross the water. Once he reached land he started walking. He walked through Texas and kept walking until he reached Spartanburg, South Carolina.

He found a job in a livery stable that paid him three dollars a month. The job came with a blanket to sleep under and three meals a day. He worked there for five years and then moved on. He stopped at a wholesale house, bought a few things, put them in a bag, and peddled them house to house as he carried a stick for protection.

Each new day brought with it a new route and he walked on and on. After about a year, he bought a pushcart and loaded it with five times more than he could carry in bag and he continued to peddle his purchased wares. He sold his wares in the daylight and slept under a tarp and a blanket at night in the woods.

After about another year he purchased a horse cart and used that in his business for a few years. He could load more items onto the cart and use it for a bed when the need arose.

After so many years of traveling, he decided it was time to buy a permanent place where he could set up his business. His small store grew until it was the biggest department store in Spartanburg.

I was nineteen when Adolf Herman came into my life. He became my mentor and the most helpful person in my life.

I worked on Saturdays from ten until ten and I got one dollar. That was a little over eight cents an hour. My lunch cost me twenty-five cents and my dinner cost me twenty-five cents. That left me fifty cents which actually gave me a net gain of only a little over four cents an hour for the work. I had to walk two miles to work that morning and at ten o'clock when I got off that night, I had to walk two miles back home or I could take a ten cent bus ride.

"If you ever go into business, never cheat a customer. Give them more than they pay for and they will come back to you again and again. If they are buying a pair shoes, put in a pair of socks as an extra item. Make them happy," were the instructions given me by Adolf.

If a customer bought a pair of pants and wanted to return the pants, first Adolf would give the customer his money back to make him feel good. Then, when the customer found another pair of pants that fit, the customer would pay Adolf again with a new exchange of money.

Adolf would buy seconds and irregulars to sell them at a good price for people who could not pay the retail price.

The best lesson I learned from Adolf Herman was customer service.

A man came into the store and I sold him a pair of shoes.

Herman had a Parker Pen that he always used and it was stolen that same day. Herman kept his pen on a little writing desk at the front and after my customer left, Herman started looking for his pen. The pen was gone so he told me the guy stole it.

"I will remember that he stole my pen when he comes back in here," said Herman.

About a year later the guy comes back in and he has Herman's pen in his pocket.

Herman pulled me over and said, "That's the guy that stole my pen. He's got it in his pocket and I'm going to get it back. Don't say anything to him."

"Okay," I said.

The man buys another pair of shoes. Herman wraps them up.

"You know when you find something out on the street that's not yours you are supposed to take it to the police department then when nobody claims it you can have it and it is yours. When you find something in somebody's store you are supposed to find out if it belongs to anybody in the store. Since you found my pen and kept it for me. I'm going to give you a pair of socks for keeping my pen for me," said Herman as he handed the dumbstruck man his wrapped shoes. That guy didn't know what the hell to say.

Each day Herman would bring a sweet potato with him to eat. He really liked sweet potatoes. He had an old coal burning, pot-bellied stove on which he would put the sweet potato to cook. On the top of the stove he placed the sweet potato. He had a coffee can, I guess it was a three pound size, that he placed over top of the sweet potato. It worked like an oven and baked his sweet potato just right. One day one of the sweet potatoes exploded. It blew his can all the way to the top of the store and sweet potatoes were splattered all over the place.

By this time in my life, I had learned to read a little. Phonics were taught to me by different people who passed through my life. I had learned by practicing reading the magazines I was selling door to door. I started writing a little, a few words and phrases now and them.

Shortly after that, I got married to Hazel Vuncannon at a minister's house in Danville, Virginia, even though we were living in High Point, North Carolina.

The girl I married was working, making twenty-five cents an hour, but she was working almost all of the time so we managed to buy groceries and rent a little two room place where we cooked in one room and slept in the other at a cost of eight dollars per month. Our groceries cost us about three dollars and fifty cents a week plus we saved about a dollar and a half to buy meat during the week because we didn't have a refrigerator. Our total grocery bill was around five dollars per week for both of us.

After another six months had passed. The old man, Adolph Herman who was about seventy-five or eighty years old, gave me a fifty cent raise. I was making one dollar and a half for the day.

The war was coming in Europe and I got a little more work. I was working four days a week, sometimes five days, which was very good.

The old man gave me another half a dollar raise making my earnings two dollars for Saturday. A few months later, he gave me fifty cents more.

A shoe store, a small chain shoe store, named Pollock's opened up in High Point where I was living at the time. I figured maybe I could go down there and talk to the manager. He offered me five percent of what I sold. I took the job.

The first Saturday, I made over five dollars which was twice what I had been making at the other place. I was also earning through the week ten dollars at my other job. That made it a total of fifteen dollars per week.

The business that the shoe store was doing was in the afternoons after the mills let out and on Saturday which was ninety percent of all of the sales for the week.

At the mill where I worked, a shift let out at three fifteen.

After I left Adolf Herman in search of a more livable wage, I worked at Pollock Shoe Store on Saturday while I was working at the hosiery mill. Most of the Pollock business was on Saturday but people going home from the hosiery mill from four to six o'clock would stop in and the sales were better during that period of time than what was sold all day. The store manager wanted me to come in after I got off work at the hosiery mill. I would change into the extra set of clothes that I had and leave the mill at three-fifteen so I would be at the shoe store by three-thirty. A lot of the times I would make as much from the shoe store from three-thirty to six o'clock as I made at the mill all day. So to sum it up, I was making ten dollars for five days and I earned six maybe seven dollars on Saturday, I had learned to sell a little bit better. I was actually making more at the shoe store that I was making at the factory.

It started snowing at around noon while I was at the hosiery mill and I had half way decided not to go to the shoe store shift. I was going to call them and tell them I wouldn't be in because there wouldn't be any customers showing up, not in this deluge of snow. I made my mind up to just go on in to work. I had to travel out in the weather to get home anyway.

I'm glad I decided to go onto the shoe store. People going home were stopping to buy rubber boots and galoshes. I made about ten dollars in the two to two and a half hours of business. I didn't sell a single pair of shoes. They were coming in there in droves. All I had time to ask was "What size shoe do you wear?" I would go get a pair of boots or galoshes, hand it to them, they would try them on, while I was getting another pair for someone else.

The shoe store stayed open until six during the week and nine on Friday. On Saturday we had to take inventory of every pair of shoes we had in the store and figure out how many pair we had sold during the week and, of course, what style so we could put an order in the mail to Atlanta to replace our missing stock. It would be about three in the morning before we could finally quit work doing what was called 'taking stock.'

The shoe store chain fired the assistant manager after I had been there maybe six months and they offered me the job with a guaranteed salary of twenty-five dollars a week. With the twenty-five dollars, I would get a nickel for each bottle of polish I sold. I would get ten percent on all of the ladies handbags I sold and they had shoes they wanted to get rid of that they called PM's for which I would get an extra dime, fifteen, twenty-five, and sometimes as much as fifty cents for each pair that I sold.

I was good at selling the PM's and with all the extra incentives, I made about five dollars extra, so I actually made about thirty dollars a week which was a fantastic thing. The manager of the store was only making thirty dollars a week.

The foreman at the hosiery mill where I had left only made twenty-five dollars a week.

Shortly after that, they fired the store manager. I tried to get them to give me the job but they told me I didn't have enough experience. They hired a man from a local shoe store who had a friend he wanted to work for him, so he let me go in order to put his friend in as assistant manager.

That left me without a job.

I also received word that my brother, Fred had committed suicide at the age of twenty four.

Fred had moved in with my brother, Lytton, and a few days later shot himself in the head with Lytton's pistol. After the funeral Lytton and his wife moved to Los Angeles, California, where Lytton worked for forty cents and hour in an aircraft factory.

1939, my daughter, Glenda was welcomed to the world. I was a father and proud of it.

I was married, I had a kid at that time, so I got on a bus and I went to Atlanta, Georgia. That's where the headquarters for the shoe store was that I worked for. I went to the office because I wanted to see Mr. Pollock, the president of the company, to see if he could give me a job in one of the other stores.

The secretary would not let me in to see him without an appointment. Of course, I didn't have one. I waited until noon. I was going to wait until he came out and try to catch him on his way out; but, he never came out because he always went out the back.

I didn't see him.

I was very downhearted.

I left and went to get me a sandwich. As I was going down the street feeling sorry for myself, I saw the Western Union Store there and I passed it because it didn't mean anything to me. I was sitting eating my sandwich and all of a sudden a bright idea came to me.

On my way back to headquarters, I stopped at the Western Union store and I filled in the paperwork for a telegram to be sent to Mr. Pollock. By that time, I had learned to read and write a little bit. I filled in the telegram telling Mr. Pollock that I was sitting in his office waiting for him. I told him I had been sitting all day and that I had come from High Point and I very much wanted to see him.

The man behind the counter at Western Union looked at it and said, "Well, by gosh, he's just across the street. Why don't you just walk over there and tell him."

"His secretary won't let me see him. I want you to send the telegram and I want to request that it be delivered personally to him, not to his secretary. He's the only one to get it."

The Western Union clerk agreed.

I went back to the shoe store headquarters and sat outside his office.

A few minutes later the boy with the telegram arrives.

"I have to deliver this personally to the president," the Western Union boy told the secretary.

She picked up her intercom announcing to the president that a telegram had arrived and that it was to be personally delivered to him

The president stepped out of his office briefly to accept delivery of the telegram and then returned to his place behind the closed door. After about two more minutes, the president opened his door stepping out to look around the room where he saw me sitting.

"Are you Stanley Holcomb? Come on in the office."

The president's secretary was so surprised that she almost fell out of her seat.

I entered the area behind the closed door and seated myself. We talked for a few minutes which allowed me to explain the situation about what had happened and why I came to see him.

"I'm surprised and amazed that you would have the ability to figure out how to get in here to see me in the way that you did. It takes effort to come all of the way down here from High Point to see me. For a man like you, we've got a place in this organization. I'll see to it that you have a job. I'll call the district manager and tell him to put you somewhere immediately," he said as he picked up the telephone.

The district manager wasn't available.

"Go back home and wait for a call there," he instructed me.

The next day the call came from the district manager.

"The assistant manager's job is open in Greensboro, North Carolina, for a little store called Boyd's if you want it."

"No problem," I answered.

Greensboro, North Carolina, was only about twenty miles from where I lived and I could take a bus over there every morning to get to work.

In two months, the manager of Boyd's was drafted and they gave me the job which only gave me five dollars more a week.

By that time, the war was getting pretty close. The shipyard was taking an awful lot of employees from Norfolk and the store there was in bad need of sales people because the Army was getting some of the men.

Headquarters told me if I would go to Norfolk, they would give me an extra penny on my sales and guarantee me fifty dollars a week plus my PM's, my polish sales, and my handbag sales. That would give me, by the time all of it was added up, about sixty dollars a week.

I took the job in Norfolk.

1939 World War II begins when Germany invades Poland.

CHAPTER 4

1940'S

I stayed in Norfolk for some time where I volunteered for the Army but they turned me down.

In the mean time Pearl Harbor was attacked on December 7, 1941, so that on December 8th the United States declares war against Japan.

A few months later I was drafted and this time the Army took me at the age of twenty-one. I went to boot camp at Camp Croft, South Carolina right out of Spartanburg.

I earned a medal for having the highest score on the rifle range that had ever been achieved in the camp with an M1 Rifle. I earned 203 points out of a possible 210 with 42 shots. 5 points was the highest you could get on each shot. With 20 shots you could possibly get a hundred if you hit the bulls eye every time. I shot 42 times and hit the bulls eye every time except 3. My little medal was imprinted with "First in First". It was a little thing and I gave it to my daughter. She played with it for a long time. I guess she lost it.

The Army gave me $22 a month and they gave Hazel $28 a month out of my pay. In addition, the Army gave Hazel $50 for having a child giving her a total of $78 a month. Out of the $22 I received, I had to pay $5 a month for my laundry. I had them take out of my pay $7.50 for bonds. I only had $9.50 for me every month. Everything else was paid by the Army except my haircuts which cost 15 cents.

When we would get a haircut we would have to go stand in line. That line would be a block long. There were usually four barbers in the shop and they would all be busy all the time. They would wait till they cut the hair of everybody in the shop then they would open the door and let ten more enter. When they finished that group of ten they let another ten enter. Sometimes you would have to stand in the hot sun for an hour or an hour and a half before you could get your haircut.

I was lucky I didn't have to wait except one time and that was the first time. When they had a prisoner, they had a goof-off that might get thirty days in the brig, that had to go to the barbershop or wherever and he would have to go with an armed guard. I had to have a rifle with me even though it didn't have any bullets in it. I would take him down to the barbershop where I would knock on the door. One of the barbers would open it and I would take my prisoner inside the shop. The next barber chair that was open took that prisoner. When the sergeant wanted a Saturday afternoon off to go to town, he asked me if I would take his prisoner down to the barbershop for him. I took the prisoner in and I was out right away. When I was taking the prisoner back to the brig, each company had its own barbershop, he would take the rifle and take me in as his prisoner to a different barbershop. He marches me in there and I'm out with a haircut and no waiting in line. That's what I did each time.

I was lucky. I never had to do KP (kitchen patrol). I never pulled guard duty the whole time I was in the Army.

My Army career was not long because I was injured during training. My injury occurred with my proximity to a howitzer explosion during a training exercise and I returned home with a disability.

The United States drops atom bombs on Japan and the United Nations comes into being in 1945.

It turned out that I was injured before I officially entered World War II, even though I felt duty bound to serve my country.

I never left the United States because I was hurt during my training and I was discharged with a disability. We trained with live ammunition and the biggest we had was a 105 millimeter gun, a Howitzer, that would blow up a whole building. I was too close to the explosion and I was shell shocked. I stayed in the hospital about six weeks, at least, and then they discharged me and sent me home. I didn't apply for a disability but when I got home there was a disability check there for me. It actually beat me home. I received a thirty percent disability and they gave me $11.50 a month, it was raised to $34.50 a month. After about a year they cut it down to ten percent which gave me $11.50. About a year later they said that I was still disabled but not enough to be paid. Then about seven months later they called me back and said they made a mistake that I should have been getting ten percent. They have never called me back for another examination and I still receive ten percent today.

The biggest bother I have from the injury is that when I move my head fast it gives me a headache. It always has. It comes from the shock that I got from the explosion. I've never been able to move my head real fast without the headache. I've been told I could go back and get it raised to one hundred percent but I've never tried.

I went back to work at Pollock's Shoe Company when I got back out of the Army. They didn't have a place to put me to start with except in Charlotte, North Carolina, so they sent me down there and gave me assistant managers pay. I had to stay in a hotel for three or four weeks.

I left Charlotte when they needed an assistant manager in Raleigh, North Carolina. They had a young girl in Raleigh who was not doing the job very well. They told me that they would hire me as the second assistant manager in Raleigh because they needed the help.

I was in Raleigh for about a month before I ever found a place. It was so hard to find a place to live.

The first thing I would do was to look in the newspaper. Any places that I called had already been rented. I went down to the newspaper and to talk to the advertisement taker. I told her I wanted to put an advertisement in the paper which was my reason for wanting to see her. Why I really wanted to see her was to bribe her to give me telephone numbers for rentals coming out the next day. I wanted to call those landlords the night before the advertisements in the newspaper were printed. That's the only way I was going to get a place to stay. That's how hard it was to find a place to live.

I got a rental that night before it was printed in the paper. The woman told me she would not permit children. Well—I had the little girl but Congress had just passed a law that any returning service man could not be put out of his home for having children. I moved in with my daughter and the landlady ordered me to move. I told her I wasn't going to do it.

She went down to the real estate board to complain. She wanted me put out on the street and they told her to get me off of the premises she would have to file a complaint. She filed that complaint based on the fact that I had a child and she didn't permit kids in any of her vacancies. They told her that it was illegal to put me out because I was a returning serviceman. She filed the complaint anyway.

The real estate board turned the complaint down and Hazel, Glenda, and I lived there about a year until they transferred me to Norfolk. After about three months the manager quit. He had been with them a long time and he was making sixty-five dollars per week as a store manager. A store manager wasn't supposed to sell any shoes unless they had more customers than the sales clerk could handle. He received only three percent for any of his own sales. They raised it to seventy-five dollars a week.

As a salesman I was making a hundred dollars and over a week. Some weeks I would come under a hundred dollars but most weeks I was making, at least, a hundred dollars or more.

I received a message from the president of the company. He was the same one that I told I was outside of his office waiting for him.

"You couldn't possibly be managing the store properly and sell as much merchandise as you are. You sell as much as anybody in the store and that's not a manager's job. You're supposed to manage the store," stated the sternly worded telegram.

"Just look at what my salary was as a salesman. You cut my pay twenty-five dollars a week to be a manager when I was making over a hundred dollars a week as a salesman.

"You can have the store back and I'll go back to selling shoes," was my equally stern response.

They didn't want to do that. They wanted me stay on as manager but just sell the overflow that they salesmen couldn't take care of which would be maybe ten dollars a week, if that much.

I kept right on selling and the next week when the figures went in I got a phone call from them.

"You can fire me if you want to. I can go right across the street and get a job making more than I'm making here as manager being just a salesman over there," I told them.

They sent the district manager to see me.

"You've got to cut that out or they are going to fire you," said the district manager.

"You can fire me if you want to but, like I told the president of the company, I can go right across the street. He has been trying to hire me. He told me he would give me a hundred dollars per week guaranteed. No—I'm not going to take a cut as a manager."

After about three more weeks, they finally found another man to take the job for seventy-five dollars a week. I went back to the seven percent commissions and assistant manager still making over a hundred dollars a week.

About a year later they needed somebody bad in Norfolk so they transferred me there as assistant manager. I made more there than I made in Raleigh. I would rather live in Norfolk.

I bought a house in South Norfolk. It was an older house and the first house that I ever owned and that was in 1946. The house had seven rooms. Half of it was two-story and half of it wasn't. There were three upstairs rooms and four downstairs rooms.

I took the top of the kitchen off and extended that and put on the front two rooms. I made it twelve rooms with four apartments in it of three rooms each. In each there was a living room, a bedroom, and a kitchen. It became a four-family apartment building.

I bought the lot across the street and built a little brick two bedroom house on it. The lot already had a building on it that I converted into a two bedroom house. It was the same property on which the brick house was built.

That's where I started my wholesale auto parts business by putting parts on panel trucks and selling those parts to garages and gas stations along the many country roads.

I needed to be different when I went calling on people. How was I going to do that?

I'm small in stature and I'm not the best looking man in the world. I'm not ugly by any means, but I'm not Robert Redford.

I'm clean and dressed presentably but I didn't want to blend in. I wanted to be different.

A hat, that's what I needed.

I got me a Stetson hat and that became my trademark; my piece of identification that made me stand out in a crowd.

I went to work selling shoes on the road wholesale to the stores in Virginia, West Virginia, North Carolina, South Carolina, and Georgia. At that time, all the little towns had a shoe store.

My new job was selling shoes as a traveling salesman because I knew I would never get more than a salary working for the shoe store. I traveled around for a few years and I did quite well selling shoes.

The travelling around constantly along with a stint in the Army wreaked havoc on my marriage. Seeing the world and everything it had to offer caused my vision for my future to change drastically.

The travelling and being away from home changed the feelings my wife had for me, too.

We worked at getting along and remaining husband and wife, but it wasn't enough. Divorce entered my mind and festered like a boil.

The newly built brick house and two bedroom rental house were what I gave my wife, Hazel, when I divorced her. I had an agreement that I gave her the house completely and with the other house on the same property as rental income, I was to pay no child support. The child support was going to come from the rent and she had the other house free and clear for herself which she was very agreeable to. Child support back in those days was very little. The rent on the house was more than I would have had to pay for child support in 1948.

Jack Dempsey retired from professional boxing during the 1940's and successfully ran a restaurant in New York. Ernest Hemmingway wrote For Whom the Bell Tolls and many southern sharecroppers migrate to war-related jobs in the cities.

CHAPTER 5

1950'S

The same year Israel was created followed by the election of President Harry S. Truman. The Korean Conflict begins officially in 1950.

1953 brought on the election of President Dwight D. Eisenhower.

In the 1950's almost seventy one percent of the farmers had automobiles, forty nine percent had purchased telephones, and ninety three percent had electricity not to mention running water.

Segregated schools were declared unconstitutional which sparked the Civil Rights Movement led by Martin Luther King. Rosa Parks was arrested for civil disobedience when she refused to give up her seat in Montgomery, Alabama.

After the divorce from Hazel was final in 1955, I needed a change of scenery.

I met the lady who would become my second wife, Clara Mayer, in 1951. Her father was the number one lieutenant for Mobster Frank Costello.

Clara and her husband owned a department store in Charlotte, North Carolina. I sold shoes to them and that's how I met her. We remained acquaintances over the years.

Clara was a tiny little thing. She weighed less than ninety pounds stood five feet tall. She was very thin with her normal weight being eighty-eight to ninety pounds. She had reddish blonde hair and blue eyes. Her voice was soft. She had a good sense of humor.

In contrast, Clara's husband was a very, very cruel person. Max her youngest son, said he saw his father beat his brother so badly that blood would run out of his brother's ears. When Max was twelve years old he told his daddy if he ever did it again he was going to kill him. There was about five years difference in their ages with Louis being the older brother.

Not long after I moved to Florida Clara came to a shoe show. I had a display there, in Charlotte. The display was in between seasons so we had a small display set up in a Charlotte Hotel. The different shoe companies, maybe fifteen or twenty, thought people might want a new style or need to fill in for the shoes that they had sold and wanted to reorder to replenish their stock. We would spread our shoes out on the bed for display. At night we would take the shoes up, put them in the cases, and sleep on the bed. The next morning I would get up and put them out on the bed again. We did this even in the big hotels in New York and Atlantic City.

A couple of styles were all Clara would buy from me because most of what she stocked were cheaper than my line of shoes. She bought them by the case because it was wholesale. She only sold women's shoes with eighteen or thirty-six to a case. Depending on how big your store was you might buy five cases of the same kind or a small store might buy one case.

Clara had a department store in the lower end of town in Charlotte. She ran the store, kept the books, and her husband sold on the outside. He would load his car up with stuff and go to colored town and sell dresses and coats for fifty cents down and fifty cents a week. He would go around every week with a load. He finally bought a panel type truck and he could haul bigger loads. When his customers would get one bill paid up he would sell them something else. It was the same clothes that they could buy in the store for five dollars and he would end up getting about twelve dollars for it. He had to charge more because he had to go by every week to collect his money. He made pretty good living doing that kind of selling.

Clara divorced her husband in 1955 and acquired two jobs where she worked as a doctor's receptionist in the day time hours and a bartender in Orlando at night.

I had already divorced Hazel who chose to remain in Virginia.

Eventually Clara and I were drawn together and we became a couple.

Clara and I decided to take the couple thing a little bit further. We were married in Valdosta, Georgia. We enjoyed our honeymoon in Florida.

Clara came into our marriage as a package deal. She had two sons, Louis and Max.

When I decided I wanted to move to Florida there was a shoe company in Lynchburg, Virginia, where I would stop each time I'd go near the place to see the sales manager and try to get a job in Florida. That was so difficult to do because after the war, it seemed like everybody wanted to move to Florida.

One morning I was traveling on the road and I had to detour at least fifty miles out of the way to go to a factory. Something told me to go there. This has happened to me many times and I knew there was a guardian angel sitting on my shoulder directing me where to go.

"I'm here again looking for a job in Florida," I told the sales manager. "Do you have one for me?"

"No, I can't give you one, but I'll tell you where one is available. You can have it if you want it," he told me.

"That's fine with me. I would certainly appreciate the opportunity,"

"Just thirty minutes ago, we hired a salesman from the International Shoe Company from the Sundial Division. The company doesn't even know he has quit. You can call them and ask for the job before they even know he has quit."

"I'll do that, thank you."

I went outside the company and dialed the telephone number of the International Shoe Company on the first pay phone I could locate.

"I would like to talk to the sales manager?" I said excitedly.

"Who's calling?"

"Stanley Holcomb."

The sales manager came on the line and I started my preamble.

"Sir, I want the job your salesman Butler has just left."

"Butler wouldn't quit us; he would never quit us. Just last month we loaned him money to buy a house. He's is too loyal to quit," he sputtered.

"All right, I tell you what. I will make a deal with you right now. If he has quit, can I have the job because I know you are in dire need of a man there. It is the change of seasons, Butler already has his samples because they have been shipped to him and your sales meeting is at the last of this month. If he has quit, how quick can you get a man to replace him? I want the job and I want to make a deal with you that you will give me the job if he has quit.

"You've got a deal," the sales manager replied.

"Okay," I added, "here's my phone number. I'm going home and I'm going to wait right there until you call me."

That conversation happened on Monday and I went home.

On Tuesday morning at about ten thirty, the sales manager called me and said, "You were right. I'm going to keep my word. I don't know you. I've never heard of you but I know you are a very resourceful person in the getting the job done; otherwise you would never have called me. Can you meet with us on Friday, at the Mayflower Hotel in Washington, D.C.? That's where our sales meeting is going to be."

"I'll be there."

I met the sales manager there and then I went down to Florida.

That year was a very good one for me.

We had a sales meeting in Manchester, New Hampshire, where the factory was that made the shoes that I sold. I traveled there arriving a day before the meeting and I checked in that evening.

I went out to the lobby at about three o'clock where I saw a gentleman sitting there and we started up a friendly conversation. He seemed to be a very nice person. Later, as we talked, I discovered that he had written a book. He took a liking to me and gave me one of his books that he autographed.

I certainly didn't have any books. I especially didn't have any books autographed personally and given to me by the author. I was so proud of that book. I didn't have time to read it before the sales meeting so I took it back to Florida with me.

I was unmarried at the time and I was dating a nurse. The nurse had a friend, a pharmacist, who was having a party that next Saturday night. He asked my nurse friend to come to his party and to bring a friend with her so she asked me to go.

While at the party, I told the pharmacist about the book. He wanted to read it. He only lived about a couple of blocks from me. I knew I wouldn't have time to read it before the next week so I said I would go get the book and bring it to him to read.

He lost the book. I never saw the book again. I would truly love to have that book. It was so important to me for some strange reason.

The end of the decade, 1959, allowed Alaska and Hawaii to be admitted to the Union. We were fifty states strong.

Shoes continued to be my way of life. I worked for the Shoe Box in downtown Orlando during the time it took me to attend school to get my real estate license. Selling was in my blood so selling real estate was an easy path for me to follow.

I flourished with selling the houses so I started buying those houses, remodeling them, making them suitable for the Federal Housing Authority who would then buy them from me.

When I tired of that, I bought an apartment building in which I resided and started building homes and installing water systems into subdivisions outside the city limits.

CHAPTER 6

1960'S

Civil Rights was the topic of discussion in 1961 when civil rights activists organized a series of Freedom Rides to protest segregation on interstate buses and in bus stations.

President John F. Kennedy was assassinated in 1963 and the Vietnam War raged for nearly ten years.

I had dinner with President Lyndon Baines Johnson in Orlando, Florida in 1964 when he was campaigning to be re-elected. The invitation was a delight.

Lyndon B. Johnson was president following Kennedy's death until 1969.

Speaking of things presidential, I slept in a room that Theodore Roosevelt had slept in the Oregon. Teddy was a hunter and fisherman and spent a night there in a tiny hotel with a wood stove.

In 1965, my mother, Bertha Rutledge Holcomb, age 85, died in a nursing home in Portsmouth, Virginia.

That same year I started a vending machine business, stocking cigarettes, coffee, and snacks. It was a lucrative business but prone to break-ins.

One machine was broken into and all the cigarettes were stolen twice for the loss of three hundred dollars each time. When one of the bigger machines was vandalized and robbed, it would cost six hundred dollars.

My second wife, Clara Mayer Holcomb, died of heart problems in 1967 leaving me alone again.

Taylor appeared in my life again when I was in Florida. It wasn't a happy reunion, not for me anyway. I never quite trusted Taylor since my childhood days and he proved to me, once again, that I was so right.

During his stay in my home he stole my television and my boat. I should have known better but he was family.

Taylor's reappearance into my life only reminded me of what I didn't like about my youth. Other than the fact that Taylor was the boy that could do no wrong which I truly didn't like, there was also the problem of the harsh religion that my father practiced.

My father, Graham, was raised as a Quaker with its very rigid rules and regulations.

I, on the other hand, was raised with a father practicing a religion I couldn't recognize. I couldn't plaster it with a label because I really didn't know what he was practicing. My thought was that it was cruel and mean. It was a religion that I didn't want to have any part of now or forever.

I researched the various studies of religion and I determined that I preferred Judaism. I converted to Judaism in 1955, the religion of my choosing.

My name in the Jewish world became S. Eli Hillel.

In 1969, at the age of 48, I married June Nolan Thacker who was 38 in Jacksonville, Florida. Again it was a package deal. June had a daughter, Linda, and a son, Dayton Lucien Thacker.

I continued to run my vending machine business and June kept books for a tire shop.

CHAPTER 7

1970'S

I moved to Florida in the middle fifties and June and I left there in 1970 going to Oregon. I looked around Oregon for a while and I decided I would go into the electric lamp manufacturing business. June and I worked that lamp business and within five years, I had built our manufacturing plant into the second largest electric lamp manufacturing plant west of the Mississippi.

June could never say "I love you" but it didn't matter to me because I knew that she did the whole time we were married. Nobody could bend over backwards any more than she did to take care of me. If she didn't care for me she wouldn't have done that during the whole time we were married. I do not remember any time, for breakfast or dinner time which was always a sandwich or supper time, that she didn't before she prepared it, ask me what I wanted to eat. For breakfast I would eat a couple of eggs, English muffin and some hash browns. Sometimes I would change and eat some corned beef hash but she would ask me what I wanted.

"Look, you've never cooked anything I didn't like. You don't have to ask. Just go ahead and cook it."

"No, I'd rather know what you want."

When we got married she wanted to make a deal with me. Whatever was to be done in the house she wanted to do it herself. The outside of the house, the lawn, shrubbery, and planting the garden (we had a nice garden and she loved the garden) was what I had to do. The inside of the house was what she wanted to take care of herself. She even wanted to take the garbage out. I agreed to the terms of the deal.

For my clothes, she would make sure there wasn't a button off of anything. She would mend them and she could fold a shirt. You couldn't tell it wasn't fresh from the factory because she folded that neatly. I've never seen anybody that could fold clothes as neat as she could and put them in the drawer.

At that time, I traveled an awful lot and each time I got ready to go on Monday morning my suitcase would be packed. I never had to check in there to see if there was anything I would need. It was in there. All I had to do was put it in the car and be confident that I had what I needed at all times.

It may have been the way she was raised, her mother and father were almost like my mother and father, two cruel people. It might have been that is the reason she couldn't tell me that she loved me.

We had made an agreement that whichever one of us died first, we would come back and let the other know that we could come back. Some people believe that and some don't. Some believe in reincarnation and others don't. If she died first, she would come back, if it was possible for her to do it.

Just a few nights after she died in 1992, I was lying on the bed, and I hadn't gone to sleep yet. She came back. I could see her as plain as day. She came up to the bed, leaned over.

"Eli, I really did love you."

That's all she said and then she just faded away. That was the only time she ever came back. That's the only time I ever heard her say those words and it was after she was dead.

I have kind of a hang up like she did. I didn't do it like some people, so mushy that they are constantly saying "I love you."

I certainly wasn't like the fellow that was traveling, selling shoes in Carolina the same time I was. I ran into him in Kinston, North Carolina. We were both checking into the same hotel and he suggested that we go to dinner that night. He told me when I got ready to come on up to his room and we would go.

I entered his room and there he was sitting on the side of the bed with a woman on his lap. He had his hand stuck up her dress and he had a phone in his other hand talking to his wife telling her that he loves her. To me that was worse than not telling her he loves her. I never will forget that.

I did go on to dinner with him that night and I wanted so much to ask him "How can you do something like that? You got that whore sitting down on your lap and telling your wife that you love her."

I would rather have been like my wife, not telling me that she loved me. I know she did. She had the utmost respect for me, my wife did and that, I think, is even better than love.

June couldn't stand to be closed in if it was dark. She didn't want to be in a tomb where she couldn't see. In a car you are closed in there but you could see all around you and that didn't bother her. Shutting her up in a closet bothered her. The dark was what she couldn't take.

We lived in the country most of the time and she liked to live in the country which she had never done before we got married. We lived in town for about the first three years and we would go up to the camp when we were getting ready to put the trailer in. We just had a little pup tent, nights without moonlight, she would be in the pitch black in the tent. That didn't bother her because it was open all around us. She loved to go camping. She had never been camping or fishing prior to meeting me. She liked to go camping by herself. I'd kid her about going back to Oregon with me. I was planning on going out there but then this thing came along with them stealing the trailer and I had to stay around close in case they needed me there. She liked to go fishing with me. She liked to go hunting with me. Eventually, we went camping, in the Ocala National Forest.

When I first went to Oregon, I went into the import business. I didn't lose money on it but I didn't make any.

After that, I opened an electric lamp manufacturing company that was very, very successful.

We stayed in a little town called Vida about twenty five miles from Eugene on the Mckenzie River. There were only a couple hundred people in the town, if that many. There was one store that had gas pumps. That was it so far as business was concerned.

In 1970, we bought a home there that was right on the side of a mountain. The back part of the house was actually built into the mountain that went straight up. Unless you were pulling on trees or bushes you couldn't get up the mountain.

We got our water off the side of a mountain. A spring came right out of the mountain to where there was a thousand gallon concrete reservoir. We had a pipe that came down to the house.

The house set off about three hundred feet from the road. There was a creek that went right in front of the house that had running water in it all year long. There was a bridge about fifty feet long that went over the creek. At the end of the bridge was my front porch. That was as close as you could drive to the house because it was on the other side of the creek.

We had a garage right out in front where the bridge was. You go across that bridge and it was part of the house.

It rained ten months out of the year. The boards on the bridge, of course, when it rained would swell up and they would stay tight. In June, July, and August, it did not rain and the boards would dry out and shrink up so that when you walked across them they would rattle something terrible.

We had a manufacturing plant where we made lamps. Along with the main building, we had three storage places for the materials.

June would go to work and assemble the lamps. She could assemble about fifty lamps a day. She would quit and go into the house to fix lunch.

On this particular day, the creek had attracted a lot of wild ducks. I went into the house for some reason about ten o'clock. When I came back out to go to the shop to assemble lamps again, I looked up the creek and there were five ducks a little way up the creek sticking their bills down in the mud trying to get bugs and stuff out of it. They were all mallards.

At about eleven thirty, June was going to the house to fix lunch. For some reason she decided to run across the bridge. She starts to run across the bridge and the boards were loose. It was in July or August, the boards were dry and loose making them rattle like everything and her running made it even louder. Those five ducks had floated on down and were right under that bridge. She started crossing the bridge making that racket, of course, the ducks went out of there quacking loud and one of them flew into the post under the bridge. She said it scared her so bad that she had to go to the bathroom. The ducks scared the living daylights out of her. She scared the ducks as bad as they did her.

Sometimes I would open the window and shoot ducks from my living room. I didn't have to go miles to hunt them and chase them down. They were right there in the creek. I didn't kill for sport. I wouldn't kill them if I didn't eat them.

When I would shoot one of the ducks, I would have to run outside really quick, get off the side of the porch, get down on the ground. It was about ten or twelve feet up from where the creek was under the bridge. I would get there as fast as possible, pick up the stick I left down there for this purpose, and start pulling the duck to the bank with the stick; otherwise, the duck would float right on down the creek and be gone.

Just beyond the house I had about a dozen apple trees. The grouse would come out there and peck the apples eating the seeds. Sometimes one of the grouse would fly up and fly right into the back part of the house. I would leave the door open on the deep freeze and they would fly right into the deep freeze already picked and cleaned. That's what I would tell people for a good laugh. I actually would go out next to the apple trees, shoot one, pick it, and put it in the deep freeze.

In the fall, deer would come out and stand there eating apples within a hundred feet of me, maybe a half dozen at a time. I killed a couple of them for food. They would eat the apples on the ground first then they would reach up as far as they could. When they had eaten all the apples they could reach, they would stand on their hind legs hitting the limbs trying to knock them off so they could eat some more apples

We ate deer, grouse, ducks, and geese, too.

A grouse is a very stupid bird. You can walk close to them. One fellow up Horseshoe Creek was fly fishing and he was sticking sticks in his rear pocket. He was going along the creek where there were quite a few grouse. He would see one, walk up to it, take the stick and hit it on the head. He would take fish and grouse home for dinner.

We dined on pheasants, too. One day just before the season opened, I was going home and there was a pheasant rooster in the road. For some reason I knew he was going to sit there until I got to him. Just as I got there, he flew up right on top of the fender of the driver side of the car, it hit him and broke his back. I stopped the car, got out, picked him up, put him in the car, took him home, picked him and ate him. I wouldn't pick one up that had been laying there but this one I killed myself.

Ring neck pheasants will stay put too until you get right at them only then will they fly up. When a dog is after them, they will fly off in front of the dog. Sometimes if the brush is thick they'll hide in the grass and wait there until you walk right up to them. If they are in a cornfield and you are walking to get to the end of the row, they'll fly when you get there. You can get pretty close to them.

Sometimes I order some pheasant already smoked and cooked but they cost about thirty five dollars. Pheasants are not real big, a couple pounds is a good sized one. Maybe at Thanksgiving or something like that I'll order one but otherwise I'm not going to pay that much for that little bit of meat even though it is delicious when smoked.

Daniel Graham Holcomb at the age of 94 died at a hospital in Portsmouth, Virginia, while I was living in Oregon in 1972.

My eldest brother, Lytton, born in 1898, passed on in 1976 as the result of an auto accident when travelling in Oregon.

It was around that time that I sold the lamp manufacturing plant and decided to move back to Virginia.

Many of the years that followed were marked by presidents. They were Jimmy Carter, 1977-81; Ronald Reagan, 1981-1989; George Bush, 1989-1993; and William J. Clinton, 1993-2001.

The little town I chose to move to was called Montvale located right outside of Roanoke. That was where I planned to live out my retirement years.

CHAPTER 8

THE REST OF MY LIFE

I had nothing to do. I sat around most of the time and was so very bored.

"Where's the Eddie Bauer catalogue that came in the mail yesterday?" I asked my wife one day as I was preparing to eat lunch. "I'd like to look at it while I eat."

"You didn't get a catalogue from Eddie Bauer," she told me.

"Oh yes I did. It had a moose standing behind some trees on the front cover. I don't know what I did with it."

"I haven't seen it," she said.

I knew if it were in the house, she would have seen it because she knew everything that went on in the house.

I ate my lunch and, about one o'clock, I walked down to the mailbox to get the mail. There was the catalogue that I had seen me getting the day before and it had the moose standing behind the trees on the cover. I took the catalogue and showed it to my wife.

"That is just another one of those things that happens to you. You see things before they happen. You saw the catalogue before you got it," she said.

The owner of the house we were living in killed himself in that same house. We didn't know it when we bought and the house. It wouldn't have bothered me even if we have known it, but we actually didn't know.

We had a one thousand foot driveway that was very steep through the woods to the house that sat in the woods. The driveway had been paved with asphalt but it was breaking all to pieces and it only lasted three years.

I decided to pave the driveway with concrete.

I was retired and wasn't doing anything so I bought a mixer. There was a gravel pit located about a mile from the house so I would be able to get my gravel, start mixing, and pour the concrete. I only poured a few feet a day. It took me all of that summer and then winter came and I couldn't pour anymore because it would freeze and bust up the concrete. I waited until the next spring to start pouring the rest of it.

I finished the driveway, a thousand feet of paved concrete that I had done by hand. I was kind of proud of it.

Many times when I was out there pouring the concrete, I would look up and Mr. Merchant would be standing nearby watching. He owned the house before we did. Mr. Merchant was the man who killed himself in the house. He stood there wearing the same pinstripe suit that he was wearing when he killed himself. I could go out into the yard and he would be standing out there, but most of the time when I saw him was when I was pouring concrete. I know I have seen him, at least, twenty times.

His wife said he loved the basement because it was very cool. In the summer I would also go to the basement because it was nice and cool. I would stay down there for a little while and a lot of times I would see him down there.

After finishing the driveway I was back to doing nothing again. I was very tired of being retired. I was thinking about going back to doing something.

"Eli, please don't go back in to business, you don't need the money. If you have to do something, why don't you just get yourself a job. Work Monday to Friday, get your paycheck, come home, and forget about it. If you're in business, you're going to work yourself to death," my wife told me.

"Okay, that sounds good," I thought.

I went to work for Lowe's building supplies, managing their home improvement department. That department had never done anything except lose money. It had never made a profit during any of the months after the store opened for business.

Immediately, I started making a profit and within ten months, it was the number two money maker in the entire chain of more than two hundred stores.

The other stores were performing so poorly with their home improvement departments that the company decided to close down all of the departments. There went my job.

I wasn't going to work on a pay scale that was worth about two hundred dollars a week.

I started looking around for something else.

A saw mill supply part company in Mississippi had an advertisement in the newspaper for a salesman. I went to Mississippi to see them. We talked.

Their previous salesman retired after fifteen years. He had never done anything to push the products. He just carried the line as a side line and he made about thirty five hundred dollars a year out of it.

They decided they wanted to put a woman in the job. They hired a woman who worked for them for six weeks. She was out on the road and she never made a single sale during that entire six weeks. The company had paid her a salary and her expenses.

"I'm not interested in a salary or expenses," I told them. "That's not the only way I would take the job. We can work out all of the small details later. I'm not trying to find out what your profit margins are, but please tell me how much it cost you straight through on the average on the sale of the merchandise."

"It cost us fifteen percent of the total sale price to produce the product," responded my interviewer.

"All right," I said, "I will take that on for fifteen percent. I'll pay my own expenses instead of working for the puny little salary that you want to give me. I'll work for you for three months and I'll pay my own expenses even if I don't make enough money to pay all of the expenses. I'll stick with it for three months. In those three months you have the privilege of firing me if you don't like what I am doing."

They all agreed.

They gave me a sheet of paper to fill out, an itinerary of where I was going, who I was going to call on, how long I would spend with each call, what they said, what I sold them; or, if I didn't sell them anything; why I didn't sell them something.

"Look, if you want somebody to fill out reports, hire a high school person or another girl like the one you hired for six weeks and paid her expenses and a salary and she never sold anything. She did fill out, I understand, beautiful reports. I will not send in reports of what I'm going to do, or what I didn't do, or why I didn't do it. I'll only send in orders. If you don't want the orders and you want reports instead, hire someone else."

They didn't like what I said but they hired me anyway.

For the first month I made over seven hundred dollars for the whole month.

The next month, I made about thirteen hundred dollars. Out of this money I had to pay all of my expenses for travel, food, and lodging.

The third month I earned about twenty-two hundred dollars; followed by thirty-seven hundred dollars.

In the fourth month, I was made the "Best Salesman in the Company Ever".

After five months, I never made less than four thousand dollars a month in commission which was more than the president of the company was making. I also turned in on the fifth month more orders than had ever been turned in by any salesman in the entire time the company had been in business which was twenty-five years.

I saw a lot of the stuff that we needed so I told the president of the company that I could sell a tremendous amount of this product very easily. Well, I found out that the president of the company would not put anything in stock or put any new product in unless it was his idea. Any idea that a salesman had, in the president's opinion, was no good. It had to come from him.

"Look, I'm not going to go out there and spend my eight hours of the day and my money traveling and pass up fifty percent of the business that's out there. I will put it in and sell it as a sideline."

That's exactly what I did and I did it well. Each time I put a product in my sideline, then he would go and put one in his stock. I never sold his and I told him I wasn't going to sell his.

"I am making two times as much profit on it as I am getting on commission. Why should I sell yours when I've got my own?" I asked him.

This kept going on for about a year after that confrontation. I was making three times as much profit off of my own product as I was his product. He couldn't stand that so he fired me.

So, good. I worked full-time selling my own products. I increased my business enough to make twice as much as I was making on commission from his stuff and certain items that he had were good. I even bought them from him and resold them at a good profit.

Within one year, I was making, at least, one hundred twenty-five thousand dollars a year with the products I was carrying. I kept on working and after about five years from when I first started, I decided to retire again and sold my business. I made four hundred thousand dollars profit.

I retired again.

The last of 1979 my wife was diagnosed with cancer. She had to have surgery and I was still working at the time, so I took a month off to stay with her during her operation and early recuperation. My adopted daughter who was eighteen years old was able to take care of her supplying her needs. Thankfully, she could mostly take care of herself by then.

I went back on the road selling again. Business was very good.

My wife recuperated very well and quickly, under the circumstances.

I decided I needed to move close to where my daughter was living in Virginia Beach. The daughter I had adopted had found a job in Richmond.

If I moved to Waverly, Virginia, I would be half way between Richmond and Virginia Beach.

I bought an old house, built in 1800. It was a large house with about forty-three hundred square feet in the interior. It did not have electricity, or baths, half the plaster was off the walls and the bathroom facilities were located in an outhouse. Nevertheless, the house was solid having been built out of heart pine, hand-hewn. The beams under the house were twelve inches by eighteen inches, and the ceiling beams were four by ten.

I completely restored the house so it would appear just like it was in 1800. I put in the kitchen twenty four linear feet of solid walnut cabinets. In the living room and the library that I built, I put in walnut wainscoting: massive fourteen inch moldings around the ceilings, solid walnut mantels climbed up the ceiling, and each room had a fireplace.

I bought a complete set of woodworking equipment because I was making all of the stuff for the house that included the walnut cabinets, walnut wainscoting, the walnut panels on the wall, and the walnut mantel pieces. I did it all myself.

I built bookcases out of solid walnut. What I would do would be to put the equipment inside the house. I started upstairs first so that when I finished all of that the equipment wouldn't be in the way. Next I worked in the rest of the house and when I ran out of space to keep the equipment and still have to repair, I built two thousand more square feet to the house where I put my woodworking equipment in order to have a place to put it to finish the main part of the house. I ended up with more than six thousand five hundred square feet in the house.

The house had no closets in it. You just didn't build closets back in those days. In some of the rooms I have two closets and in some I have only one.

The rooms, all of them except one up stairs and one downstairs, are twenty feet by twenty feet. They are large rooms.

I covered the floors with oriental rugs, real thick wool oriental rugs.

The house has a front and back stairway. The front hallway to the house that goes all the way through the house and out through the back is fourteen feet wide upstairs and downstairs.

When I bought the house, it had seven outside entrance doors to the house. I can enter the house from the north, east, south, or west.

Norman Sisisky, Congressman, State Senator for eighteen years, and United States Congressman for fourteen years was a member of the temple with me in Petersburg, Virginia.

Sisisky's son, Terry, and I fed street people downtown. There would be one hundred thirty to one hundred forty people each time we fed them. We fed them in churches using their facilities. A lot of the street people wouldn't remember where to go so maybe the first week, the first day it would be down to sixty people; then each day as they learned where we were feeding them, it would build right back up again to the larger numbers.

The money came from Terry and my pockets. I bought them each a Whopper from Burger King. Terry brought cookies, potato chips, and a soft drink from Sam's Club.

I spent more than ten thousand dollars for food for them over ten years. We fed them eight times a year, every ninety days. Terry and I would feed them two consecutive weeks, four times a year which would be eight times a year. The churches would take over and feed them when we didn't. A lot of the times all the church would give them was a little bowl of soup and a cup of coffee and call that a meal.

The churches would be set up with four or five rows of tables. Terry and I would go there before twelve o'clock, put the potato chips, cookies, and the cold drinks on the tables. At twelve o'clock, we would open the door and let them enter. We would hand each one a hamburger as he came through the door.

A few of those who came in there were absolutely not homeless with some of them employed as government workers.

Terry handed out the burgers and I seated them. If I didn't seat them they would scatter out all over the place. I made them fill a table at a time. If they were coming in too fast we would hold them up at the door and I'd help Terry. If we didn't have enough help and we needed, at least, four workers total, the ladies from the temple or churches would pitch in giving us a helping hand.

One day I got the Chief of the Nottaway Indians to help. His name was Walter Brown. I filmed one of the chief's yearly pow-wow's and it took all day.

In late 1984, there was a movie being made in Richmond, Virginia, starring Richard Chamberlain. They were looking for extras for bit parts. I went up and applied for it. I didn't tell my wife that is what I was doing. About three weeks had passed and I hadn't heard from them.

We were sitting down to eat the lunch she had prepared for me and I told her what I had done.

"Ha! You think you're an actor. Really? You really thought you were going to get a job acting in Richard Chamberlain's movie?" she said between the bursts of laughter.

"Well, I could try. That's all I could do."

We both laughed about it and before I finished eating my sandwich the telephone rang and it was the movie company. They called and told me that I had the job which consisted of a small part. I took that small part. I was quite interested in it.

I met a guy who made commercials. He was very friendly and I talked to him garnering all of the information I could get. I started making commercials.

All total I have probably been in two hundred fifty commercials from newspaper, magazine, television, billboards, and what have you.

I also was in a few more movies with a few of your known stars like James Garner, Jack Lemon, a few people like that, including Mary Tyler Moore.

Another movie was being made in Richmond for which I applied and received a major role. I had the best role, the leading role in it, and the most time in it of anybody in the movie. I received a very nice write up about me in the Washington Post.

In 1988 during this movie making time, my wife was stricken with cancer for the second time.

I was very active in the Ruritan Club where I was on the District Cabinet Board but I had to resign because I felt that I should stay home with my wife and take care of her.

My wife lasted for four years and, finally, in 1992, she died. Her body had wasted away from the ravages of cancer. She weighed fifty seven pounds when she died.

I decided to go make some movies of my own. I went to California where I knew a guy out there that was making movies, directing, and writing. I asked him to write a script for me and asked him to direct the movie in which I co-starred. We made the movie in California, mostly around Stockton.

After I had been back in Virginia for about a year or so, I decided to make a movie about Nat Turner. I made a movie of Nat Turner's life from the beginning of the day he was born until the day he was hanged. I produced and directed the movie and I also played a small part in it myself. The role I had played was of a plantation owner who was the original owner of Nat Turner.

When I decided to make the movie about Nat Turner, it was announced in the newspaper. Within one hour from when it was published in that newspaper I received a telephone call from a man who had known me for more than seventy years.

"Eli, if you bring a camera into Southampton County to make a movie about a bunch of niggers, I will see to it that you are run out of the state and never permitted to re-enter. I have already talked to every supervisor of the county and they have all agreed that you will not be permitted to put a camera on any property of the county. You will not get any cooperation from the county whatsoever."

I received several calls from other people. Some of those people were threatening my life, some of them were just calling me a nigger lover and what have you.

Most of the people in Southampton County are very good, kind, decent people. There are less than a dozen of them that really gave me a hard time.

In 1968 or 1970, I forget which year it was, Twentieth Century Fox had set aside four and a half million dollars to make the same movie I made.

They went into Southampton County and started shooting the movie. They were given such a hard time, that after spending a million dollars on the movie, they pulled up stakes and said forget it. We're leaving and that is just what they did.

My friend Gene Burdick, a neighbor at one time, was having some electrical problems and feeding her horses at night was proving to be difficult. She called an electrician and he quoted her a price of six thousand dollars to do the repair work. I went into the attic of her house and helped her fix her problem. She was ecstatic when I switched on the lights. For six months she kept calling me and feeding me dinner.

"We are on this earth to learn lessons," Burdick says. "Eli is a fascination to me but not all people are like Eli. I was rushing out of the house in a hurry one day when Eli came by my house."

"I'm making a movie and I need to shoot a background of a wood fence around a house," he said in explanation.

"I don't care. Go ahead and shoot."

"I'll be happy to pay you."

"What for?"

"For using your property."

"For crying out loud, Eli, there is no cost to you," and she drove out of her driveway and I drove in. I needed a wooden fence for my movie about Nat Turner during a period of time when there were no metal fences.

Gene adds, "In spite of three heart attacks, Eli has still not stopped having fun in life and doing lots of things. Eli does not look at people as if they are Indians or Chinese, et cetera. They are just people. We would sit on my back porch many an evening and have dinner. When I had the flu, Eli would place jars of chicken soup and Matzo balls in my mail box. When I got better, my brothers teased me about Eli being my boyfriend, but it was never like that. We were good friends. I went to a few hunt clubs, fish fries, and chicken fries with Eli. I love dancing so he treated me to a night out occasionally."

I shot the movie on location, as much as I could. One person let me use his farm for the scenes. He received a bullet hole through his office wall warning him not to let me shoot any more movies on the property; however, he wasn't intimidated.

He told me I could shoot the movie on his property and I went back out there and continued shooting the movie.

I obtained a permit to carry a pistol in my pocket in case I attracted too many problems. The person issuing the permits for business in Southampton County was a very, very nice person. He did everything he could to help me.

"I can't find any place in this office that says you have to have a license to shoot a movie in Southampton County. Let me talk to the county administrator and see if we can come up with something," said the clerk.

He called me a few days later and asked me to come to see him.

"She can't find anything and neither can I. However, I'm going to make a suggestion to you. The permits for business in this county are run according to how much money you make in your business. It costs somewhere between twenty-five dollars to five thousand dollars. Now, what I'm going to put in it is that I do not believe you are going to make any money on this business so you can qualify to buy the lowest permit you can buy. It will cost you twenty-five dollars and I think it would be a wise investment. If you're on the job out there and the police come out there harassing you, show them your permit and tell them to get lost," he told me with sincerity.

I bought the permit.

I visited the county courthouse to obtain the locations of some of the houses that I could not find where Nat Turner's group had raided during his insurrection.

"The courthouse of Southampton County does not have the address of any single piece of property in the entire county," I was told by a dutiful clerk.

Of course, I wondered how they sent out tax bills if they didn't have any addresses.

I was not permitted to look in the books to find the locations at all.

I would have a crew of people dressed like slaves out in the fields picking cotton while we were shooting the film. A group of people would come by with their cars when they found out where I was shooting. They would start honking their car horns and making so much noise that it was difficult for me to shoot the picture. However, I put up with it and I went ahead and finished the movie. It took me a bit longer than expected.

While my pick-up truck was parked and we were out in the field shooting and picking cotton, something ran into my pick-up and bent one of the fenders up pretty bad. That's the worst that happened to any property that I had while shooting the movie.

I obtained the services of the same screenwriter that wrote the movie I shot out in California to write the screenplay for the Nat Turner movie. His name was Leo Fong. He had written about twenty successful screenplays and had six or eight of his own movies that were successful.

An editor in Richmond, Virginia, whom I had met, wanted me to make a movie about people who had been reincarnated.

I wasn't too fancy on reincarnation because I didn't exactly believe in it although I didn't disbelieve. I was straddling the fence over that one.

I saw an article in the newspaper about a lady who was regressing people to their past lives. I called her and she agreed to regress me. I went to her house and she tried to regress me back to the day I was born but she wasn't able to do it.

"Sometimes things work and sometimes they don't," she said.

She did get me back to where I was eight years old. I was living in Missouri in a little, log cabin very similar to the one I was born in only it was smaller. I was out in the yard and I was wearing some old ragged knickers pants as they used to call them. I was feeding the few chickens we had. In the regression, my mother was in the house and her health wasn't too good. She was a very heavy woman while my father was a tall, skinny guy who was seldom home. He was always off drunk somewhere. We barely had enough to eat but we managed to live.

At another time, I visited her and she regressed me back to when I was twenty-nine years old, in Missouri. I was a First Lieutenant in the Confederate Army. I was standing on top of a little knoll looking over the valley. The war was almost over. Down in the valley behind me where my fields were and just beyond that to the right was a little one-room log cabin where I lived alone before the war. In the field were four Confederate soldiers. They had two mules and a wagon and they were picking corn out of the corn field. I had given them permission to have the feed to give to their mules to eat. That was the last time that I regressed.

I fully believe in reincarnation now because twice I have been taken back and I could see myself as plain as I see myself here right now.

The lady that regressed me was a very nice, kind lady who name was Patricia Walker. I called her up on the telephone a few years ago to talk to her for few minutes and she was very glad to hear from me. She wondered what had happened.

The idea of making a movie about people who were reincarnated, never came to fruition. I never did make the movie.

I met a man named John Boyd, who was the president of The Black Farmer's Association of America. They were starting to try to get money from the government for the wrongdoing that they had been done and discrimination against them for getting loans for black farmers. This was a very hard trip for him and he was just getting started. He asked me if I would make a movie of the events. I told him I would.

We came together on a price. I charged him just what it cost me. I didn't want to make money off the discrimination against them. I shot it at his house out in the central part of Virginia. Part of it was shot down in Carolina and part of it was shot at a chicken house at his home. Actually, most of the movie was shot in Washington, D.C. on trips that I made up there when they were having hearings in the Agricultural Department auditorium where Glickman would preside over the meetings. I shot many hours of it there. Of course, I had to edit it down to two hours. Over the several trips that I made up there, I got some nice stuff on it. They still didn't have the money to pay me for it. They did give me a little bit but that was all. I produced and directed this movie myself.

They wanted a second movie made, a short one of another trip they were making up there. They were taking a mule and walking down the sidewalks in front of the Justice Department protesting. They were hoping to get justice for the injustice that the government had been doing to them.

"Okay," I told them. "I'll go up and I'll make this one, a thirty minute one, that's all I'll do. I'll produce and direct it and I won't charge you anything for it. It will be a free gift to you. Whatever it costs me will come out of my pocket."

They were very grateful.

I went up and I made this movie for them of thirty minutes of their complaints up there. Shortly after that, the government admitted they had done wrong, very wrong since back in the eighties and they agree to pay them hundreds of millions of dollars. It might even go into the billions to pay off the farmers for the injustice and the money they caused them to lose, the farms they caused them to lose simply because the government had discriminated against them which they agreed to correct. They settled on an amount of money that the judge approved and they got paid off.

John Boyd, the man who had me make the movies, got a five hundred thousand dollar settlement for his part. He and Linwood Brown who had also received a settlement of an unknown amount, came over to see me. I believe Linwood Brown's settlement was a little smaller than John Boyd's but I don't know for sure. They gave me a check for everything that they had promised to pay me for the movies that I had made for them.

In 2003, I sold the Virginia plantation house that June and I had restored. I no longer needed or wanted such a huge amount of living space.

PART II

CHAPTER 9

FROM THE BEYOND—AND NOT

I have experienced the presence of guardian angels all through my life. I recognized them in all forms as they came to me.

Jimmy, the Senator's son was a customer in my parts business. He was very wealthy owning more than one hundred fifty thousand acres of land. When I wanted to sell my business, I went to see Jimmy to ask if he knew anyone who might be interested in buying it. He asked me to wait for a day or two and he would let me know something. The next day Jimmy came to see me with a deposit to buy the business and asked me to stay and help him for ninety days paying me five thousand dollars to do so. My guardian angel had told me to go and see Jimmy.

Many times my guardian angel asked me to call some interesting people in the news items of the paper. When I called, they always helped me in some way.

There came I time that I wanted to buy a Fifth Wheel, a camping trailer, but in order to do that I had to purchase a truck to pull it. I had to sell my car to get this idea into motion. I put an advertisement in the newspaper and managed to do all of the tasks I needed to do and get myself on the road. I saw the hand of an angel here without a doubt.

During my childhood, I can recall the influence of my guardian angels.

I was not aware of the guardian angels when I was really young but around the time I reached twelve or fourteen, I started recognizing them and the role they played in my life. Some unseen strength would pull me towards some things and away from others. This made me wonder about other beings or powers.

When I was a small boy my father beat me regularly. When I was five my father told me he did not like the buckle on the belt that he used. I was such an obedient and somewhat smart boy who taught my father how to fix the buckle. My father fixed the buckle and then beat me some more with it. If I cried he would tell me, "Stop the tears. Dry them up or else I will give you more crying."

I would go sit in the barn or go to the woods so no one knew where I was.

I have never seen my guardian angel so I can't describe her features. She directed me well throughout my life. My life has been reasonably happy and successful in spite of my rough beginnings. I have accomplished many of things that I wanted to accomplish.

I feel that whenever something good might happen, she whispers to me telling me to go ahead and do it giving me instructions on when and where to go. I listened, so good has happened.

I was walking by the colored cemetery that was between my house and the town of Ivor on a full moon night. I heard a noise over where the grave yard was on the left side of the road, a grinding type noise. I looked over there and I could see something come up in the air. Two, three, or five seconds later it would come up again and I could hear the noise. I was scared. I couldn't move. Finally, I took off running as fast as I could.

I found out what it was that I was running from under the full moon. It had been extremely hot, about a hundred degrees, that day, at least. They were going to bury a man the next day. In those days you dug a grave with a shovel. This colored man was there digging that grave, making noise, and throwing the sand out of the grave. That's what I could see come up and just disappear. That scared the heck out of me.

Some people say I'm psychic but I really don't think I'm psychic.

I have known of strange things happening all around me at different times.

A retired colonel, Roger, in Smithfield owned a bed and breakfast called Four Square, three miles away from their home. The colonel's wife died of cancer. A friend's wife, a widow named Hager, joined him to run the bed and breakfast. They traveled around in their Air-stream trailer.

I used this property for my movie "Nat Turner."

Roger's deceased wife knew Hager from their time in Gettysburg.

Roger insisted he did not believe in ghosts.

One day when they were coming home from a trip, there was no power anywhere in the nearby homes. There was a light in the workshop behind one of the houses, and Hager pointed that out to him. When he called the power company they said it was not possible.

This event made him rethink his disbelief in ghosts.

Roger's friend, Hager, bought an old house about two miles down the road from Roger. The house looked all chopped up because additions had been added haphazardly. Hager talked about ghosts that were all over the place. He had a lot of Civil War time guns. On the third floor in one room a gun would be placed next to the door. Hager would put in back where it belonged and he would find it next to the door again. His wife was afraid of the strange happenings. Other things were also found to be in different places after having been moved from the original settings. Roger's wife had had enough of the strange occurrences and left Roger without looking back.

PART III

CHAPTER 10

WHY?

I have felt through the years that even though I didn't get much of an education and that I was raised hard with only the bare necessities being met; I didn't have to turn bad by learning to rob, cheat, and steal to get what I wanted out of life. Instead of following the path to destruction, I worked at making myself a smarter, better person so I could support my family well enough and not consider myself poor. Being poor isn't wrong; it was just that I didn't want to be poor; not anymore.

An example of how people can do wrong took place a few miles from where I lived in Virginia. A crane is a huge monstrosity of a machine that has to be loaded up, in most cases, onto a trailer and towed to its destination. The size of the machine prevents it from being driven from location to location as you would do for a smaller vehicle.

Well—now I know this is hard to believe but someone, maybe more than one someone, loaded that monster up and stole it from the work site.

That is a sample of someone doing the wrong thing by choosing the wrong path to follow.

I told the businessman that I knew where his crane was stored. That businessman offered me a thousand dollars to tell him where it was and I refused to take the money. I did tell the businessman where the crane was located after I had checked it out myself. The businessman's son had stolen the crane and wanted to sell it for some petty cash.

From my own personal experience, I had a book stolen from me. It happened to be the only book I had ever received signed by the author and I was so proud of it. A friend of a friend borrowed it and it was gone for over forty years.

The book came back to me, I don't how or when, but I found it in my house laying on a table for all of the world to see. That was a good feeling to find that book and eliminate the bad feelings I subconsciously held for the borrower.

The book episode was one of those paranormal type events that occurred in my life for which I have no logical explanation.

Another such occurrence happened when Ted Lange, the actor who portrayed the bartender, Isaac Washington, on the TV Series "Love Boat", contacted me. He wanted help to make a movie about the historical figure and slave, Nat Turner.

When Ted Lange arrived in Southampton County, I gave him a tour explaining the events that had occurred in the surrounding area as related to Nat Turner.

After Ted Lange had departed, he called me indicating that he had left his camera under the seat of the rental car he had been using. He asked me to identify the camera to the car rental manager so that I could retrieve the camera from them and send it to him.

I consented to his request, contacted the car rental office, and told them I would be there to look for the camera. Much to my dismay, the camera was not under the seat of the car. I was disappointed when I returned home knowing that I would have to call Ted Lange and tell him the camera was still missing.

I went searching for Ted Lange's telephone number and was shocked when I found the camera in plain sight on the buffet in the dining room in my house.

Over the years I have met many famous people.

I am proud of say that I have known more than twenty senators, congressmen, and governors.

In my capacity as magistrate, I have had the honor to marry couples and unite them for a walk to their future.

For my religion, I have conducted Hebrew services.

My father's religions were many. All were based on what he wanted to say about them and not anyone else's words. I was taught that other religions were sin holes. That is to say that other religions other than the one that my father was practicing at the time were sin holes.

I could not understand his ideas. "Ask and you shall be given", going to hell by believing or not believing, were not concepts that I liked. The Catholic religion was never to my father's liking. He liked Baptists and others a little.

Later in my life, in my business line, I met a lot of good Jewish people. I felt that if there was a religion that was right for me, it was Judaism. Any religion that tries to teach good behavior is fine. The Book of Ethics is a good one to read for everybody.

I was impressed very much with the Jews in Florida when I was running a few of my different businesses. They taught me a lot about integrity. They treated me ten times better than the Gentiles did. They trusted me to open an account. They treated me like Adolph Herman did.

I had never had any religious guidance from my family in life in my studies, or religion, or anything. There is a saying in another culture, that a boy was raised by the wind. I could have become a criminal, robbing like a hobo, jumping on freight trains, and living in shacks. Again, some invisible guardian angel helped me and kept me going towards a better future.

In the beginning of the year 2006, I decided to celebrate my Bar-mitzvah. Rather than at thirteen years old, I was eighty five when I started taking classes at a small temple where there were some students, older than me, too.

When I was in Florida, my stepson, Max, and I celebrated my Bar-mitzvah at Temple on the 11th day of February, 2006.

A major turning point in my life was my converting to Judaism. I would have to say it was the biggest one of my life. My whole world changed. The type of people that I associated with changed. Some of the people that had claimed to be my friends, when they found out that I was Jewish, turned their backs on me. Of course, it is my feeling that a friend doesn't do that.

He was no friend of mine anyway. He was just a phony. I'm better off without him was the way I had to look at it.

My life has led me to many varied paths, but I have always made good choices, I hope.

When I first married, I was earning twenty five cents per hour. That successful undertaking led me to many other jobs and I remained successful in business until I was eighty eight years old. At that time, the president of a company in which I had invested embezzled 1.2 million dollars; most of the money being mine. Through this company, we were buying houses, 84 pieces of real estate, to turn into a money making venture. Several months had passed before I discovered that the property was transferred to family members and sold with the profits never being seen by the company.

The man who perpetrated the embezzlement is being investigated by the federal authorities for mail fraud. I was told to use the state legal forces to prosecute my former friend and embezzler for bilking me out of my hard earned money because the state would act much faster than the federal authorities enforcing the prosecution.

He was paying $10,000.00 per month on the interest but taking the principal to pay bills so the company assets were depleted in a matter of months. He teased me constantly about the fact that he needed all of my money so he could retire. I should have taken him at his word.

The investigation has uncovered the fact that none of the chattel mortgages were ever registered with the court system for the 84 properties that were received and sold.

This investment, my last one, proved to be my only bad business investment during my long business career.

I have worked for and owned many businesses during my active years and they each and everyone proved to be successful. I made most of my money by selling the businesses that I had started.

I give my mentor, Adolf Herman, credit for the guidance he instilled in me from the first day I worked for him selling shoes.

My basic theory for customer service is and was that when the customer needed certain items on regular basis, I would buy those items in bulk and undercut the competitor's price by offering better customer service with having those products on hand and in my rolling stock whenever possible.

If there was a mistake made, I would make every effort to correct it at my expense by devoting the necessary time to facilitate the correction.

My customers appreciated the extra effort on my part.

When I started selling parts to the sawmill businesses, I would visit each sawmill in my territory every three months. Many of the owners/managers of the sawmills didn't want to change dealers because of the loyalty built up over the years. Many of the sawmill people had been working with their dealers for twenty or more years.

Nevertheless, I continued to call on those businesses trying to earn their trust and letting them know that I would be around, regardless.

By the third time I called on them, I had earned a little of their trust because I carried most of the items they used on my truck. This stocking move allowed the buyer to avoid freight charges not to mention that the product cost less and was immediately available.

I used to visit a sawmill in Maryland where the man who ran the place told me he can't buy from me. When I asked why, he said it was because of poor service.

I corrected the problem by asking him to tell me what he wanted and providing it for him on the spot. He then became a regular customer.

When one of my customers didn't pay or, at least, made arrangements with me to take care of the late payment, I would have to tell him he couldn't buy anymore until he paid up or satisfactory terms were reached.

In the same company where I was working as a salesman, I discovered that if I told the president what I needed and it wasn't his idea, then he didn't do it.

His idea of customer service was for the customer to pay in thirty days. Many of my customers needed sixty days to pay and they would receive a nasty, threatening letter after only thirty days had elapsed.

The customer showed me that letter saying he didn't want to buy from us anymore, telling me not to come back again.

I decided he didn't say that I shouldn't positively return so the next time I thanked him for talking to me and giving me a little of his time. He was a little bit friendlier and I wasn't barred from the premises.

The next time I called on him; he bought something. It took effort and patience, but I finally won him back to buying from the company.

I always treated my customers like they wanted to be treated—with respect.

If I had to order something for the customer, I would have it shipped to me and save the customer half of the freight charges. Every little bit helped the customer and helped me maintain that customer as active.

Many times my wife would field the calls for me acting as order taker, researcher by looking up the name of the machine in the catalog, and calling the factory to get it shipped to me on the next bus that traveled to the area closest to my home.

On a Saturday, my day off, a new customer called needing saw teeth, a size that he couldn't locate anywhere else. He became a regular customer.

A gentlemen called and explained that just before closing he had fired a guy who got so angry that he threw a crowbar into the wood chipper breaking the many parts.

I had some of the parts but not the complete set.

Well—I got to thinking about how I could help this man keep his business going. I had a cousin in Natural Bridge, Virginia, who had parts that he could loan the customer because they were not in use at his facility at that time. I picked up those parts in Natural Bridge and delivered the borrowed parts to the needy customer.

The happy customer bought two complete sets of parts, one to replace the borrowed parts, and a spare set to have on hand.

Another of my customers needed a grinding wheel stone. My predecessor had promised delivery for eight weeks.

I called W.W. Grainger who had the stone in stock. I received the stone and delivered it to the customer the following Monday morning. He was so pleased that I had found the stone and delivered it to him that he placed all of his future orders with me.

My rules for business:
Use common sense.
Be there regularly.
Go get the business.
Offer the best price.
Furnish the best customer service.
Make sure you have the product available.
Customers will come to you. You don't have to go to them if you offer quality and service.
Buy in bulk to save on shipping and receive lower prices.
Reduce prices for resale.
Eliminate competition with better prices. I could sell for less because my overhead wasn't as great.
To be successful in business one must get a product that a lot of people use. You must have a lot of competition, too.
If you have a product that has no competition, then you have a product that no one wants or needs.
If you sell retail, you must give your customers a good product at a good price and a good service. They will come back for more. A one-time sale is what you will have if you cheat your customers. Do not mark the product too high. Stack them high and sell them cheap.
You cannot go broke making a profit. You can and will go broke if you price your products out of the market.
If you are selling to a retail store, make sure you sell merchandise that he can resell and make a profit. He will be happy to see you on your next selling trip.
If you manufacture a product, you must cut every corner without cutting the quality in the product you are manufacturing.
Here are some examples of a successful business tactic.
On a street there are twelve businesses. Ten of those businesses are selling oranges and two of the businesses are

selling apples. I would go for the business of selling oranges. A good business is where there is healthy competition, not one that has no demand. Go for the oranges and offer a good price, good service, and honesty, but don't sell for too low a price that can make you go broke.

When I was handling real estate, one man came to Virginia from Minnesota and bought a eighteen hundred acre farm with a beautiful house and its twelve foot high ceilings. He returned to me every winter following his purchase of the farm and bought a few more foreclosures. He owned thirty houses by the time he died.

If you treat people right, they will come back to you and this man from Minnesota proved that time and time again.

The first holiday that I can remember celebrating was after I got married to Hazel. I couldn't do much to celebrate a holiday because I didn't know what they were. Those things were completely unknown to me thanks to my father. It was good thing he didn't work for the government because of the many holidays they observe.

My first holiday celebration was Thanksgiving in High Point, North Carolina, with her family, if I remember correctly.

We got married in the fall and Thanksgiving was not too long after that.

Hazel was the first one in her family to get married. She had an older brother and he got married shortly after we did. There was no fancy furniture, just a plain table, a dining room wooden table, not fancy in any way with plenty of food including turkey and the trimmings along with the vegetables and what have you. It was big family, twelve all total. Hazel had half sisters. When Hazel's mother was pregnant, Hazel's father kicked her mother in the stomach. That kick killed her mother. Her father had done the killing a long time before that Thanksgiving dinner and he had married again.

The only thing I helped with at that Thanksgiving Dinner was filling my stomach. The women in those days did all of dishes. I don't know of any men back in those days that helped with kitchen work, cooking, or housework, or whatever had to be done.

The men sat around and talked. I didn't smoke at that time. I was about thirty three or thirty four before I ever started smoking. Then I started smoking cigars. There was just nothing there in cigarette for me.

My first Christmas was in December 1938. I think we had it at home or at Aunt Lily's home that was where we rented two rooms. Aunt Lily had other people living there that included her old maid sister. Lily's husband had drowned and Lily took in boarders. She rented one room to woman named Hattie, a school teacher, and another room to a school teacher whose name I can't remember. There were five of us all total. Hattie had never married and she was about thirty years old, an old maid spinster; but, about a year later she got married.

Hazel put up a tree. It wasn't much of a tree. We went out riding down the road where we went into the woods and chopped a tree down. We couldn't afford to buy one. I forget whose land we stole it from. We went to Woolworth's five and dime where we got tinsel. I think that's what you call it. It's made out of lead and looks a little like strings of tin. They quit making it because it was made with lead. Kids were eating it and getting sick. You could buy a package of it for a nickel. We bought two or three packages of tinsel and bulbs. I think they cost probably about a quarter a dozen. All of the tree trimming items cost us less than a dollar. I'm sure of that including the angel we put on top of the tree. We put a sheet underneath it to look like snow. We couldn't afford to buy cotton to go under there although it wouldn't have cost very much.

In High Point it did snow, at least, once every year, I'm sure sometimes two or three times. I can't remember if it snowed at Christmas.

Christmas wasn't exciting to me because I was taught that you shouldn't celebrate those holidays. It really wasn't too exciting for me.

It wasn't a big celebration because we didn't have money for a big celebration

When you're taught as a kid something, you believe it, from birth to sixteen or seventeen continuously taught something, it stays with you for a long time. You don't know any different. You were never told anything different so you really don't know.

I didn't know if God would be angry with me for celebrating Christmas. People were telling me we should celebrate Christmas. I'd been taught that you shouldn't all my life. I was right in the middle.

I really didn't believe it and, yet, I did believe it. I was taught one way and then, all of a sudden, I'm hearing it another way. I wondered which way was right.

I would never have had a Christmas tree if not for Hazel and June. I grew up with the idea that it was just make believe and you shouldn't have one.

Some people tell you that Jewish people have a Hanukah bush. There is no such thing.

There was an old lady not too far from us who owned a bed and breakfast. She thought she knew everything about Judaism but she didn't know anything. All she knew was what she heard somebody say or told her and they didn't know what they were talking about in the first place. Whatever she would hear somebody say that was the gospel truth. She would go around and repeat it. Some of it was true, of course, but a lot of the stuff was not true.

The first Christmas gift I bought for somebody was for a girl thirteen years old that lived about a mile from me through the woods. I was fourteen years old. We were sweethearts in 1935. I bought her a genuine pearl necklace. It wasn't make believe. It cost me ten cents and I knew it had to be genuine for it to cost ten cents from Woolworths.

She lived through the woods. If you cut through the woods it was about a mile. If you followed the road it was over a mile. Her family had two boys and one a little younger than me and the other a little older. I would spend Saturday night at his house and let one of the brothers come spend a Saturday night with me. The older boy was Julian, the younger one was Clifton, and Elsie was her name.

About a year later her father moved the family about twenty five miles away. All we had was a horse and buggy except for Byron who had an old Dodge. We didn't have any money to buy gas. When she moved twenty five miles away it was like being on the other side of the world because I had no way to get there. I never saw her after that until I moved back to Waverly in 1983.

Julian had moved away and then came back to Ivor which was about seventeen miles from where I lived. He told me his mother, his daddy's second wife was living right out of Ivor on Highway 460 in a trailer. She had always been good to me so I went by to see her. She was glad to see me. The second time I stopped by there to see her, June and I were coming from Virginia Beach, she wasn't home. We were just getting back in the car when Elsie, the daughter, drove up with her in the car. That was in 1983 maybe. I hadn't seen Elsie since 1935. It had been forty eight years. Elsie's husband had died and I never met her husband. She lived in Smithfield and she came up to see her mother quite often she told me. I had forgotten about it, that I was the first boy that ever bought her a gift, that necklace, so I guess she was my first sweetheart.

I was at the doctor's office in Suffolk and his technician was doing a cardiogram on me for the doctor. We were talking and I said something about Elsie Phelps.

"How do you know her?" she asked me.

"We lived about a mile from each other in the middle 1930's," I told her.

"That's my grandmother," she said.

I asked her about Elsie. I hadn't seen Elsie since that one time when she brought her mother home. She told me she was in a nursing home at Windsor.

I stopped by to see her. I took her a little bouquet of flowers that I bought at Walmart. She had been there about a year at that time. She was so weak that she couldn't hold a pen in her hand. June had been dead several years so each time I would go through there I would go to Walmart, buy a vase and then buy flowers to go in it. Elsie appreciated those flowers so much. When you get old nobody wants you. She appreciated the flowers and the visit.

One bunch I bought had a red rose in it. One of Elsie's friends who would come up and sit with her a few times a week said that the red rose was Elsie's favorite. She was so weak you had to get right down in her face almost to hear her speak and she told me that was her favorite flower. After that I would take a half dozen roses in a vase to her.

I would tease her by saying, "I'm going to Florida where it is nice and warm. Do you want to go with me? I'm going next Tuesday. You be packed and I'll pick you up."

She got a kick out of me teasing her like that. She had all of her faculties and was still a beautiful woman. She was eighty some years old then. The last time I was there a lady from Smithfield was walking down the hall. She saw me and called me over to her and went back to the room with me.

"I don't know if you can get her wake or not. She sleeps about twenty hours a day and she is so weak it is almost impossible to hear what she says," the Smithfield lady told me.

I am very proud of the fact that I was asked and was very willing to conduct services in my chosen religion.

I have traveled on four continents, North America, Europe, Asia, and Africa. I have visited forty eight of our fifty United States, with only North Dakota and Alaska not being traveled by me.

I am now ninety years old and I have lived a good life.

PART IV

THE TIME LINE FOR THE HOLCOMB/HILLEL FAMILY

AND SELECTED WORLD EVENTS

1877—President Rutherford B. Hayes elected.

1875—Constitutional amendment is drafted by Susan B. Anthony or Elizabeth Cady Stanton to secure votes for women.

1878—Stanley's father, Graham Holcomb, was born in Yadkinville, North Carolina, and raised as a Quaker. Yadkinville and Yadkin County were originally farming communities with flue-cured tobacco as the major cash crop.

1878—The amendment for women's vote is introduced in Congress.

1879—Thomas Edison invents incandescent light.

1880—Hybridized corn is produced.

1880—Stanley's mother, Bertha Rutledge, was born in Yadkinville, North Carolina.

1881—There were 17 tobacco factories in operation in Yadkin County. The county commissioners delayed industrial development of the area due to repeated decisions in the mid to late 1800's not to allow railroad construction in Yadkin County.

1881—James A. Garfield, a Republican President.

1881—Chester A. Arthur, a Republican President.

1885—January 11—Alice Stokes Paul, legendary feminist, is born on a 214 acre farm in Moorestown, New Jersey.

1885—Grover Cleveland, a Democratic President.

1889—North and South Dakota, Montana, and Washington admitted to the Union.

1889—President Benjamin Harrison, on Ohio Republican.

1890—Idaho and Wyoming admitted to the Union. Massacre at Wounded Knee, South Dakota. Cream separators come into wide use. 40-50 labor-hours needed to produce 5 acres of wheat, 35-40 labor-hours needed to produce 2-1/2 acres of corn.

1891—Development in southern Yadkin County was delayed until the railroad was extended to Mocksville. Railroad line construction brought prosperity to the north side of the Yadkin River in Surry County.

1892—First gasoline tractor built by John Froelich.

1893—Grover Cleveland, a Democratic President.

1895—June 24—William Harrison 'Jack' Dempsey was born in Manassa, Colorado. George B. Seldon is granted U.S. patent for the automobile.

1896—Utah admitted to the Union. Spanish American War. Rural free delivery is started. Farmers come to town less often, but stay in touch with the world and economic conditions better.

1897—President William McKinley, from Canton, Ohio.

1898—Stanley's oldest brother, Lytton, was born in Yadkinville, North Carolina.

1898—Prices for agricultural commodities begin to rise creating the "golden age of agriculture" lasting until 1918.

1900—Next to the oldest brother, George, was born in Yadkinville, North Carolina.

1901—President McKinley is shot by an anarchist and Theodore Roosevelt becomes president.

1902—Oldest sister, Laura, was born in Yadkinville, North Carolina.

1903—Wright brothers fly first airplane at Kitty Hawk, North Carolina.

1904—Brother, Clifford, was born in Yadkinville, North Carolina.

1905—President Theodore Roosevelt, New York Republican.

1906—The radio becomes a significant part of rural life. "The only thing that can make us give up our radio is poverty. The old radio is the last thing moved out of the house when the sheriff comes in," said Will Rogers.

1907—Holcomb family moved to Virginia where Graham raised peanuts and corn.

1907—Oklahoma admitted to the Union.

1908—1917—Country Life Movement—Industrialization and immigration begins to restructure American society.

1908—Brother Hudson was born in Sedley, Virginia.

1908—General Electric patents the first electric toaster.

1909—William Howard Taft, a Republican President.

1909—NAACP (National Association for the Advancement of Colored People) founded as The National Negro

Committee by Ida B. Welles-Barnett, W.E.B. DuBois, Henry Moscowitz, Mary White Ovington, Oswald Garrison Villiard, and William English Walling in New York City.

1910—Hudson, 2, killed when a gate fell on him.

1911-1916—Dempsey began boxing in small mining towns of Colorado under the name of "Kid Blackie." Stanley's brother, George, was a sparring partner for Jack Dempsey.

1912—New Mexico and Arizona admitted to the Union. Amedeo and wife, Louise, founded Planters Peanuts in Suffolk, Virginia. Mr. Peanut mascot was born.

1912—Holcomb family moved to Nebraska where Graham raised wheat.

1912—December—Miss Paul (Alice Paul) comes to Washington, rents a basement room, and opens the office of the Congressional Committee. Two months later, she stages a suffrage spectacle unequaled in the nation's capital, taking advantage of festive arrangements for Woodrow Wilson's inauguration. Paul coordinated a march of over eight thousand college, professional, middle and working-class women in costumed marching units carrying banners.

1913—January—President Woodrow Wilson, a New Jersey Democrat.

1913—Sister Dorothy born in Nebraska near the Platte River.

1914-1918—World War I—Embattling 28 nations, embracing more than 9/10ths of the world's population. (The Lincoln Library of Essential Information, 1961)

1914—Lytton, 16, left home.

1915—Brother Fred born in Nebraska near the Platte River. Fred was born deaf but eventually learned sign language but never speaks aloud.

1916—Albert Einstein proposes the General Theory of Relativity.

1916—George left home and worked in the gold mines in Nevada. George made friends with J. Paul Getty and Jack Dempsey.

1917—United States declares war on Germany—Selective Service creates the Draft. Virgin Islands are annexed.

1917—Holcomb family moved to Virginia.

1917—January—Suffrage pickets, known as The Silent Sentinels protested in front of the White House with banners and slogans demanding the right to vote. They became the first group in the United States to wage a nonviolent civil disobedience campaign. Arrests of picketers began in July. Alice Paul is convicted and sentenced to prison at Occoquan Workhouse in Virginia. November 15, 1917, under orders from W.H. Whittaker, Superintendent of the Occoquan Workhouse, forty guards went on a rampage with clubs brutalizing thirty three jail suffragists.

1918—Brother Byron born in Sedley, Virginia—Graham buys a plot for family burials in Sedley.

1919—Jack Dempsey beat Jess Willard for the heavy weight title and then got the name "Manassa Mauler."

1919—Brother Taylor born in Sedley, Virginia.

1919—May and June—Congress passes the Susan B. Anthony Amendment which is ratified by thirty six states within a year.

1920—Panama Canal is completed. Movie houses become common in rural areas. 18th amendment prohibits sale of alcohol. 19th amendment gives women voting rights.

1920—Holcomb family moved to Missouri. Laura, 18, went to work for a phone company in Cleveland and married Mr. Diebold, the inventor of a machine that made a seamless copper tube.

1921—First Miss America Beauty Pageant held in Atlanta, Georgia.

1921—April 2—Stanely E. Holcomb born in a log cabin in the Ozark Mountains in Missouri near Long Lane Town.

1921—Warren G. Harding, a Republican from Ohio.

1922—Brother Earl born in Missouri. He dies at age of two weeks.

1923—Calvin Coolidge, a Republican President.

1923—Miss Paul drafts and introduces to Congress The Equal Rights Amendment which prohibits discrimination based on sex.

1924—Taylor hits three year old Stanley on the head with a bucket of horse manure.

1924/1925—Holcombs moved to Southampton County near Ivor, Virginia. Stayed in house rented from Mr. Brantley one year then moved ¾ mile to another house where sister Nancy (Ruth) was born. (In 1831, Southampton County was the location of the most serious slave rebellion in United States history. On August 21-22, 1831, the infamous Southampton Insurrection, led by slave Nat Turner, resulted in the deaths of fifty eight whites and an unknown number of blacks. Turner and his followers were captured, tried, and twenty were hung.)

1926—September 23—Jack Dempsey is defeated by Gene Tunney and loses his heavyweight title.

1926—Holcomb family moved four miles away to other side of Ivor, Virginia. Brother Daniel born. Graham burned up five year old Stanley's slingshot.

1927—Dempsey and Tunney fight a re-match which Dempsey loses. Civil War breaks out in China.

1928—Otto Rohwedder introduces bread slicing machine.

1928—Holcombs moved to Suffolk, Virginia, when Graham rented a farm owned by three sisters. One of the sisters, Suzie Rabey, took Stanley, 7, to town and had his ringworm treated. Graham beat Stanley and took away his new pants. George returned from Nevada in a Cadillac covered with $10,000 worth of silver trim.

1929-1939—The Great Depression—President Herbert Hoover, and Iowan Republican (1929-1933).

1929—Stanley, 8, taught a turkey to have respect.

1930—13% of all farms have electricity.

1930—Stanley's sweet potatoes spoiled under manure pile.
Stanley woke up circumcised.
Stanley learned an hour contains sixty minutes.

1931—Holcomb family moved to other side of Suffolk, a mile from town where Stanley and Byron saw their first cartoons in a Sunday newspaper. Graham burned the newspaper.

1932—Laura and her husband took Stanley, 11, and the other children to Virginia Beach Stanley rode in the rumble seat of the V16 Cadillac. Laura's husband gives Stanley and two brothers five dollars each to bring in firewood.

1933-1945—President Franklin D. Roosevelt, a New York Democrat.

1933—Holcomb family moved to Southampton County. Stanley, 12, wondered what a county was. Taylor cheated Stanley out of cotton money. Brother Fred committed suicide in Oklahoma. He had moved in with Lytton and used Lytton's pistol to shoot himself in the head. After the funeral, Lytton and his wife moved to Los Angeles,

California, where he worked for forty cents and hour in an aircraft factory.

A sheriff brings an order for Nancy and Daniel to attend school. Stanley is followed by a ghost.

1934—Dorothy left home and married a man in Portsmouth. Byron, 16, left home and went to Chicago. A black boy stuck a pitchfork prong through Stanley's toe while picking peanuts and moving vines. Graham refused to let a doctor treat Stanley's infected foot. Graham gives Stanley, 13, two acres to plant for himself, and Stanley makes eighty dollars profit off a cotton crop.

1935—Social Security Act provides retirement insurance.

1935—Stanley, 14, sneaked into theater in Suffolk, Virginia, and watched his first moving picture, *Buck Jones*, a western. Stanley has a sweet heart named Elsie Phelps, 12.

Taylor, 16, steals and hocks mother's wedding ring for 50 cents before leaving home. Stanley drives Byron's car in his sleep.

Stanley, 14, plants another crop that is destroyed by a rainstorm. Taylor cheats Stanley out of his previous profit with Graham's help.

Taylor works for a tire company in Suffolk where he sells tires and pockets the money.

1936—Holcomb family moved from Ivor, Virginia, to Winston-Salem, North Carolina. Parents told fifteen year old Stanley he could not come with them. Father sells Farm to Stanley's Uncle Elwood. Stanley works for Mr. Sadler, pulling weeds for twelve hours each day or five days, earning a total of $5.25. Stanley leaves to find his oldest sister, Dorothy, in

Virginia, but after three days leaves to find his aunt in Yadkinville, North Carolina.

Stanley, 15, stayed with his aunt for three weeks until she found him a job through the newspaper want ads for magazine sales. Stanley traveled with a group selling magazine subscriptions through North Carolina, South Carolina, Georgia, Florida, Alabama, Mississippi, Louisiana, Texas, and to the headquarters at Chicago, Illinois, before he quit.

1937—Stanley, 16, sold restored vacuum cleaners with brother, Lytton, who had a house in High Point, North Carolina, for six months until Lytton took a job with Sears and Roebuck in Danville, Virginia.

The day Lytton left, Stanley got a job at a hosiery mill that lasted six months. Stanley hitch hiked back to parents' house which was six miles out of Winston-Salem, North Carolina. Graham and Bertha didn't have a phone, radio, or newspaper in the house. Unable to communicate with them, Stanley wondered what his reception would be like. Needing help to cut wood with the two man cross-cut saw, Graham let Stanley stay for two weeks until the job was done.

At 4 PM Graham took Stanley beside the house and said, "Your mother and I had a talk and we decided that we raised you long enough. You'll have to go."

Stanley walked to the mail box and was pleasantly surprised to find a card to himself from hosiery mill at High Point asking him to return to work immediately.

1937-1938—Stanley worked two jobs, one as a clerk at the hosiery mill for twenty five cents an hour, three or four days per week and the second job as a clerk in a dry goods store for Adolf Herman, a Russian Jew, on Saturdays.

Stanley, 17, and Hazel Vuncannon, 19, married at minister's house at Danville, Virginia, but lived in High Point, North Carolina.
Boll weevil epidemic affects cotton crops.

1939—Stanley quits working for Adolf Herman and becomes a shoe salesman at Pollock Shoe Store on Saturdays.

1939—World War II begins when Germany invades Poland.

1940-s—Jack Dempsey retires from professional boxing and successfully runs a restaurant in New York. Ernest Hemingway writes for "Whom the Bell Tolls" Many southern sharecroppers migrate to war-related jobs in cities.

1941—Pearl Harbor is attacked on December 7, December 8, United States declares war against Japan.

1941—Stanley's daughter, Glenda, is born. Stanley volunteers for the Army and is rejected.

1942—Stanley, 21, is drafted in the United States Army. One of his jobs was escorting prisoners to get haircuts.

1944—Becomes disabled due to injury from proximity to Howitzer explosion during Training. He returns home.

1945-1970—Change from horses to tractors leads of second Agricultural Revolution.

1945—United States drops atom bomb on Japan. United Nations forms.

1945—President Harry S. Truman, a Missouri Democrat.

1948—Stanley starts a wholesale auto parts business, putting parts on panel trucks, and selling them to garages and gas stations on country roads.

1948—Israel is created.

1950's—Many rural areas lose populations.

1950—Korean War.

1951—The Louise Obici Memorial Hospital is a gift to the community in memory of Louise. (Planters Peanuts Founders)

1951—Stanley, 30, begins to wear Stetson hats. Stanley meets Clara Mayer at a shoe show in Charlotte, North Carolina.

1953-1961—President Dwight D. Eisenhower, a Kansas Republican.

1953—Stanley, 32, thinks about divorcing Hazel. Stanley goes to Leesburg and Orlando for the International Shoe Company.

1954—70.9% of all farms have cars, 49% have phones, 93% have electricity.

1954—Brown v. Board of Education decision, segregated schools are declared unconstitutional. This event sparks the Civil Rights movement led by Martin Luther King, Jr.

1955—Clara Mayer divorces her husband and gets a job as a doctor's receptionist and a job in a bar in Orlando.

1955—Blacks boycott buses in Montgomery. Rosa Parks is arrested for civil disobedience when she refuses to give up her seat on a bus.

1955—Divorce between Stanley and Hazel is final. Hazel stays in Virginia.
Taylor moves in with Stanley for a while and steals the television and Stanley's boat.

1955—Stanley converts to Judaism and takes the name of S. Eli Hillel. Eli marries Clara Mayer in Valdosta, Georgia. They honeymoon in Florida. She has two sons, Louis and Max.

1956-1957—Eli works downtown Orlando for the Shoebox. Eli goes to school to get real estate license. He does well in sales and remodels house for sale to the Federal Housing Authority.

1958—Eli lives on West Colonial Drive in the apartment building he bought. Eli builds homes and puts water systems into subdivisions outside city limits.

1959—Alaska and Hawaii admitted to the Union.

1961—John F. Kennedy, a Democratic President

1961—Civil Rights activists organize a series of Freedom Rides to protest segregation on interstate buses and in bus stations. (Supreme Court had already ruled segregation unconstitutional, but the rulings were not being enforced.)

1963—President John F. Kennedy assassinated.

1963—Lyndon B. Johnson, a Democratic President from Texas.

1964-1973—Vietnam War.

1965—Eli had dinner with President Lyndon B. Johnson.

1965—Bertha Rutledge Holcomb, 85, dies, at Portsmouth, Virginia, nursing home.

1967—Clara Mayer Holcomb dies of heart trouble.

1969-1973—Richard Nixon, a California Republican.

1969—Eli, 48, marries June Nolan Thacker, 38, in Jacksonville, Florida. June has two children, Linda, 6, and Dayton Lucien Thacker. Eli has a cigarette vending machine business and June keeps books for a tire shop. June's sister and parents ostracize her because she marries a Jew.

1970—United States invades Cambodia.

1970—Eli and June move to Oregon. Eli owns a lamp manufacturing business where he and June work.

1972—Daniel Graham Holcomb, 94, dies at hospital in Portsmouth, Virginia.

30303030300

1974—Gerald Ford, a Republican President.

1975—South Vietnam surrenders to North Vietnam.

1976—Lytton gets killed in freak car accident in Oregon.

1977—President Jimmy Carter, a Georgia Democrat.

1981—President Ronald Reagan, a California Republican.

1989—President George H. W. Bush, a Texas Republican.

1993—President William J. Clinton, an Arkansas Democrat.

1993—June Holcomb dies of cancer in Richmond, Virginia. She weighed fifty seven pounds. June visits Eli after death.

2001—George W. Bush, a Texas Republican.

2003—Eli sells Virginia plantation house he and June restored.

2009—Barack Obama, an Illinois Democrat.

2011—April 2—S. Eli Hillel/Stanley Eli Holcomb, 90, and still going strong.

THIS BOOK IS DEDICATED TO:

DONNA & JACK

DREAMA & BUFORD

PATTY & RANDY

MAY WE ALL LIVE TO BE
90 AND STILL GOING STRONG

OTHER BOOKS WRITTEN BY LINDA HUDSON HOAGLAND

FICTION

CHECKING ON THE HOUSE
DEATH BY COMPUTER
THE BACKWARDS HOUSE
AN AWFULLY LONELY PLACE

NON-FICTION

QUILTED MEMORIES
LIVING LIFE FOR OTHERS
JUST A COUNTRY BOY
WATCH OUT FOR EDDY
THE LITTLE OLD LADY NEXT DOOR

Would you like to see your manuscript become a book?

If you are interested in becoming a PublishAmerica author, please submit your manuscript for possible publication to us at:

acquisitions@publishamerica.com

You may also mail in your manuscript to:

**PublishAmerica
PO Box 151
Frederick, MD 21705**

www.publishamerica.com

CPSIA information can be obtained at www.ICGtesting.com
Printed in the USA
LVOW080537170112

264142LV00001B/27/P